Climate Therapy

Trust Revolutionary Wisdom

Michael J. Cohen

**How to create 54-sense moments in natural areas
that transform problems into love.**

**The Organics of Applied Ecopsychology in Action
Educating, Counseling and Healing in Natural Areas**

Project NatureConnect

P. O. Box 1605, Friday Harbor, WA, 98250
1-360-378-6313   nature@interisland.net
www.projectnatureconnect.com
Janurary 2020. First edition.

Contact us, above, to special order this book in quantity discounts.

Donations appreciated. Non-Profit Organization 501(c)(3)
http://projectnatureconnect.org/donations

NOTE: The information you gain from this book can be applied toward an accredited CEU or academically transferable course, certification, or degree via www.ecopsych.com/LNE.html.

Author Information: Michael J. Cohen, Ed.D., Ph.D. While developing the art of his hands-on science, the Organic Application of Ecopsychology, since 1953, Mike has achieved several Master's and Doctoral degrees, written 12 books and directed sensory university environmental education and outdoor education courses and degree programs. The founder of Project NatureConnect, for decades he developed and lived in natural areas on year-long, *utopian community*, environmental education expeditions. Recognized as a Maverick Genius, he received the Distinguished World Citizen Award and conceived the 1985 International Symposium *'Is the Earth a Living Organism,'* His programs consist of applying a 54-sense love-of-love in natural areas whose truth strengthens arts and sciences and additionally makes them a critically needed ecotherapy. Here, enlightened editing and contributions by **Dr. Stacey S. Mallory** improve it.

Please visit *www.ecopsych.com/mjcohen.html* for more information.

Dedication

With appreciation to all you beautiful Revolutionary Wisdom Expedition fiduciaries.

I would like to thank Everyone who has added to my learning and lifelong contribution to the Applied Ecopsycology field. As I glance back at my history, I am profoundly grateful for my life in Earth.

For about a century I, and others, have validated the information within this book. Particpants span the United States and numerous nations throughout the world. The work we each do to incorporate the processes in this book has been a framework for many individuals to add to their vocations and every day contact with Nature.

You make the world a better place to live and give me hope that the future of humanity depends on us mutually supporting each other and our home in Nature.

We thank you with all of our love, appreciation, and consent for us to be part of your journey.

There is a voice that doesn't use words, listen.
Be drunk with love, for love is all that exists.
The universe is not outside of you. Look inside
yourself; everything that you want, you
*already are. ~ **Rumi, 1250, A.D.***

Foreward: Revolutionary Wisdom

The scientific core of *Climate Therapy* is the key, globally announced truth of January 1, 1925, the environmental basic of our personal and social life. Moment-by-moment, the life of the Big Bang Universe/Nature/Earth (UNE), creates its own, self-balancing, time and space to live in. The "now" essence of each and all UNE things is a self-organzing, unifying oneness. Simultanously, as UNE loves to live its now life, it is identically each of us and our thoughts feelings and relationships living our lives now.

On August, 21, 1965, in the wilds of the Grand Canyon, Arizona, I reasonably determined that the only difference between UNE and *me/humanity* was that *I/we* could speak, think and relate with word-stories and UNE *could not.* I validated that my spoken or written, self-evident facts from 54-sense contact with UNE in natural areas could heartfelt convey how the life of UNE works. I had unknowingly become a UNE instrument, its tool or ambassador. This book shares these UNE truths so others may benefit from their coalescing process.

-- We live in, not on UNE. Whatever happens to UNE happens to us and vice-versa, from quantum to wholeness.

-- When our half-truth stories or abusive ways excessively disconnect our lives from UNE's caring balance, they disturb the integrity of our personal, social, and environmental relationships. The loss of this love makes things deteriorate, in and around us.

-- The remedy for our excessive detachments is the revolutionary wisdom of *Climate Therapy*. One attractive step at a time, it connects us with UNE's self-correcting power to remove the roots of our problems as we enjoy their antidotes in natural areas.

-- We suffer because in Industrial Society, on average, 99% of our thoughts, feelings, and relationships we manage and condition our lives to be *out of tune* with the balancing essence of UNE's dance. We lose contact with the love of its/our life to be diverse, pure, cooperative, fair and balanced and not produce garbage or war.

-- When added to anything, *Climate Therapy* (CT) connects us with UNE's otherwise omitted organic remedy for our trespasses and their miseries. This enables us to think, sense and relate as part of Albert Einstein's unified field. CT is the balance and beauty of nature around, in and as us when we visit an attractive natural area.

Contents

Introduction: The Director's Workshop

Natural attraction is conscious of what it is attracted to.

Twenty years ago, at the start of the new millennium, the Board of Directors of a Spiritual Philosophy Union asked me to teach them the art of my 54-sense, revolutionary expedition science in a one day workshop with them on Orcas Island, Washington.

The Spiritual Philosophy Union is an international organization with members and schools in 70 countries and 90 locations in the United States. It includes all forms of Theosophy and dedicates itself to investigate the unexplained laws of nature and these powers in humanity through the comparative study of religion, philosophy, and science. I didn't know then or now much about Spiritual Philosophy or the organization. For this reason, I have changed the group's name here to protect them and myself if I accidentally misrepresent them.

The Directors, who were engaged in a wide range of disciplines, requested me to present my workshop because one of the Spiritual Union's members was an online student of mine. He was enthusiastic about the special contribution my organic application of Ecopsychology makes in reversing the root cause of the problems that are causing the world to fall apart, especially resource depletion and climate change. I learned this remedial process while living 26 years of my life in the climate of pioneering utopian outdoor Revolutionary Wisdom Expedition groups (RWE) and as part of my doctoral research in natural area community building.

RWE works because it centers around its participants discovering and growing balanced, constructive relationships as they learn to discover and trust the science of their greatest truths (GTT).

NOTE: *I scientifically define and explain GTT in later sections of this book.*

The Director's workshop was held in 2000 A.D., and the falling apart of the world has increased by 30% since then. This catastrophe insists that I publish its *Climate Therapy* RWE remedy here, now. Consider this example of how RWE adds GTT in a natural area and helps us actualize a statement from the Spiritual Philosopher, Rudolf Steiner:

> *Love is higher than opinion. If people love one another, the most varied opinions can be reconciled - thus, one of the most important tasks for humankind today and in the future is that we should learn to live together and understand one another. If this human fellowship is not achieved, all talk of development is empty.*
> *~ **Rudolf Steiner***

Here's how an RWE-GTT participant's natural area experience has conveyed this knowledge and put it to good use.

"Thoughts of my life arose within as I was hypnotized by the tranquil sounds of the gentle counseling brook and attractive energies of the paradise-green trees. In this therapeutic, now moment, the chanting of the brook is eliminating the inner and outer noise of nature disconnected stories. It speaks of *limitations* in a positive fashion. I have followed and struggled with nature disconnected careers, relationships, and life paths, requiring qualities that I possessed in *limited* quantities. I now march to a different tune, reaching out with the essence of Nature's love in nature connected paths, with increased confidence, worth, and greater ease."
~ RWE participant interaction

With a Ph.D. of knowledge in hand, in 1960, I developed my organic, RWE form of Ecopsychology with others and continued to live it in natural areas year-round. This was decades before Ecopsychology became a recognized field of study. I spent 16 of these 26 years in nature that consisted of GTT evidence-based, year-long revolutionary wisdom expeditions (RWE) in 84 different habitats. In an updated way, I continued this process online in 1986.

In the climate of RWE, we scientifically explored balanced, 54-sense relationships with Nature from Newfoundland to California while we camped out through the seasons. To me, the value of the heralded, but unscientific, wilderness experiences of many spiritual and indigenous leaders seem to pale in comparison to my now sixty years of RWE study.

Without adding today's advanced RWE science, our past outmoded or limited observations and experiences tend to hurtfully sidetrack us until we update them today with evidence-based GTT. That is what I do in *Climate Therapy*. This book provides RWE answers to the many questions that were asked at the Spiritual Philosophy Union workshop and since then. It also empowers you to participate in RWE online and/or real-time locally.

Each answer that my narrative offers often includes my experiences and responses to earlier questions that I have already addressed. In addition, as in the Rudolf Steiner example, I include raw GTT quotes from RWE email participants that share their natural area interactions while on an online RWE.

A Board Member at the workshop asked *"Why do you say RWE was utopian? How could there not be any problems on an expedition?"*

The RWE groups were *ideal* because we created space for hundreds of GTT meetings in natural areas that let the life of Earth itself 54-sense teach us what we needed to know in the moment. We practiced what we learned from our roots in the natural world's wisdom. As I describe in my 1972 book, *Our Classroom is Wild America*, this is how and why our 24-person, co-ed group, was so successful. An extensive two-year study by the National Audubon Society, in 1977, identified it as the most *"revolutionary school"* in America, and educators that evaluated it called it *utopian*. Overwhelmed, some of them said: *"I learned more than I wanted to know."*

> "Everything is happening at a natural pace. Nature accepts the seasons, climate, and weather. Trees do not protest against the rain. The sun does not rebel to shine. The stars don't weep for

being in the sky. Nature has its natural manifestations. Quiet and stormy, but natural. I followed the attraction of the place. My feet felt the area. The young spruce impressed me with its energy. It was already taller, but still at the beginning. It seemed to have a lot of fresh energy. It reminded me of new beginnings. New, beginning, bright, I miss a lot at the moment" ~ **RWE participant interaction**

As a 54-sense RWE (6), the school GTT discovered and engaged in how the life of our planet peacefully organizes, regulates, and corrects itself. We created moments in natural areas that taught us to become part of Earth's *homeostatic optimums* of life, cooperation, diversity, balance, and beauty that do not produce garbage, abuse, or war.

We lived and enjoyed the climate of Earth's truths that our 54 natural senses registered so we could think and relate like the unadulterated life of Nature and Earth work. We experienced that a natural, moment-by-moment, space/time reality equilibrium exists, and its helpful process could be responsibly enjoyed in natural areas, at home, or school informally, or as organized internet courses.

Being evidence-based, RWE scientifically made sense as it let Nature's 54-sense climate transform Earth's miseries into love. It actualized the GTT in our personal and collective life. By validating 54-sense self-evidence, we experienced how the life of Earth's well-being empowered us to think, feel, and relate in greater unification with the natural world and each other.

> "As my sadness arose, it attracted other senses to balance the sadness with appreciation that I could feel accompanied by sensing joy and contentment, so I was content with my sadness. In Nature, there is a rhythm between frustration and patience that is shifting more toward patience and compassion. Each day I find moments to share this teaching, and as I do, it becomes a natural extension of who I am." ~ **RWE participant interaction**

Like it or not, today, whenever we omit the nature-connecting quest of RWE, our Earth misery abusiveness, trespasses the natural world, and problems continue, personally and globally. This book serves as a ticket, via the internet, to join an RWE remedy that our/your warped ego and society have withheld from all things (26). See <www.ecopsych.com /LNE.html>

Just as sure as you know that the person behind your eyes is UNE as you, you can be sure that, by omitting RWE, high-tech human life, including your life, has created and continues to create our climate of destructive madness that is increasingly making the world fall apart today. In 20 minutes or less, RWE empowers you to walk off that battlefield and into a supportive RWE foxhole that you build and own. It is a safe place and a GTT healing remedy for our abusiveness. You happily become the antidote for what ails us as you apply it to yourself and others. As your foxhole extends itself, the battlefield becomes smaller.

> "I love how you connected while inside. You let society's story that would tell you this was cheating open up your senses. We can GTT connect while not in the most nature-filled space, and we are changing our thinking stories and persevering as nature connected beings! Great job. I love that your cat sensed what you were doing and brought another connection right into your lap!"   ~
> **RWE participant interaction**

Our excessive separation from Nature produces
our disturbing loss of nature's love.
*~ **Michael J. Cohen***

Bridge the separation gap. Sooner or later read this book to the essence of any natural area or thing that is attractive to you. Often you can identify its balancing essence by removing its name or label, as is true for yourself, too.

The Power of Photographs

Workshop Member*: Everything has more than one meaning and since science can't prove things are actual, how can RWE make things real?*

This book presents a remarkable unification truth that blends together all things and enables us to organically manage and mend the destructive relationships that we suffer in our self, society, and nature.

Sadly, we learn to be so prejudiced against unification truth that our bias unifies us to demean, abuse, or kill each other over who owns it. *Climate Therapy* adds to our every relationship a unique Revolutionary Wisdom Expedition (RWE) process that helps us remedy this tragedy because it identifies and addresses its stem cause. It works because it uses the art and science of this unifying truth and its *Golden Sequence* to transform our prejudice against it into the love of unifying with it and each other.

To our loss, we frequently overlook, omit, or mistrust important truths because we think that they may be unbelievable, hearsay, or a lie. Photographs can help rectify this problem. For example, a person can say they were never at a certain place until a valid photograph is presented that shows them being there.

To include the power of photographs here, I use a seemingly imaginary but very advanced RWE movie camera that, in reality, helps us see what truths we are missing. Its hi-tech lens and film register up to 78 facts of life on each film frame (54 senses + 24 RWE truths.)

See <www.ecopsych.com/mindread.html>

I insert this camera image (🎥) in the text to note where in our minds we can photograph and preserve any RWE truth I present here, a truth that I and others have experienced many times. The camera brings it into focus and play so we can trust it. This affirms that the truth is authentic because I and others have registered and validated it with our 54-sense (Appendix A). The camera is one or more of the undeniable 24 facts of life. These facts have been continuously reliable. In addition, the 24 facts of life have been scientifically peer-reviewed and published (Appendix B). Best still, the camera's therapeutic outcomes are helpful with respect to reasonably dealing with our climate of unreasonable abusiveness.

For example, I point the RWE Camera-78 to this paragraph:

🎥 A powerful but hidden scientific truth in the sentence that you are now reading is identified by at least nine different truths about the sentence. They include 1) you are reading it here, 2) I am writing it here, 3) we are in different times and places, 4) we come from different backgrounds and experiences, 5) 1-4 are self-evident, undeniable realities that our senses register and experience, 6) we are unified and share the truth of #5 in this sentence, 7) this unique truth is happening, so it obviously exists as part of our lives and 8) if we repeat 1-7 next week this truth will still be evident because it is an essence of how the climate of the Universe/Nature/Earth (UNE) works. 9) 1-8 is evidence that makes this truth scientific, trustable, and accessible.

🎥 To notate this special truth, along with the truth of what you are reading now in this paragraph, I capitalize it as its proper name, **Truth**. Our personal life exists through this UNE Truth. We similarly capitalize our name because we are each have a special way of being. What is special is that this Truth is the, '*often missing*,' whole Truth and nothing but the Truth, so it helps us.

🎥 Hopefully, you directly experienced that an extra unifying force, the Truth in the 9-fact paragraph above, is working, yet the sentence does not identify it. We don't see it because we are taught to ignore it. Its Truth blends together the *nine phenomena* in the sentence and unifies us in its balanced reality. However, most of us don't know what this Truth is, where to find it and, once identified, how to use it to help us unite and solve the great problems in our personal, social and environmental climate. The whole truth is that these troubles exist because we *omit this great Truth.* As a result, we produce our runaway abuse, lies, and disorders.

🎥 It is challenging, but reasonable, to recognize that the RWE eco-arts and science of UNE Truth is available. However, it is not officially recognized, no less applied in our society. Our life experiences the loss of Truth and suffers accordingly. This explains why our history of good intentions and advanced human knowledge has ended up producing today's increasingly dangerous ways and contributed to the falling apart state of the world. This state of being includes our abusiveness, emotional pain, and deteriorating sanity.

> The Truth in this moment is that our senses reasonably register that we both know and trust that you are experiencing these words right now as you read them. This is a legitimate fact that we can validate by repeating the experience, as you are now doing in this new time/space moment. We may also discover that we are ignoring the the individual letters in these words that you are reading until I bring this to your attention; now you can see them. Yet it was single letters that were of prime importance when, as children, we began to read. You will probably discover that this single letter phenomenon will stop shortly when your habitual form of of reading takes over. Is it happening right now? If so, it is Truth.

> An additional, often overlooked Truth in this moment, includes that the words *the* and *of* were doubled in the previous paragraph and that you are probably paying attention to the black color of this ink, not the whiteness of this page. Also, you place value on the words here themselves, not on the spaces between them.

Other obvious facts not being registered include the presence of space and air between you and the page and that the end of your nose is also part of the picture, no less the glasses you may be wearing. We can discover this Truth as we help our senses of reason, trust, consciousness, contrast, time, literacy, color, distance, motion, and sight come into play in this moment.

Note: There are far more than our five senses. As we support, register and validate the sensibility of these additional senses, we seldom deny the Truth they contribute.

Lest this all seem petty, think about what happens to your internet relationship with the world when you overlook the truth that you have omitted a single dot that was needed in a webpage address, or that there is deceit in one of your most treasured relationships.

PAUSE for a moment.

Now: Think about the *singular life of each UNE space/time moment.*

Sadly, tomorrow, our mentality, interactions and management will increase our hazardous exclusion of the Truth in how we think, feel and relate while we hope and pray that things will get better. Doing the latter is a cover-up because it omits the Revolutionary Wisdom (RW) of us peacefully unifying by engaging in the available 54-sense/24-fact Truth. True hope includes a commitment to *not* exclude or warp UNE Truth.

Hope lies in the fact that the Truth of Climate Therapy helps you act, enjoy and benefit from its powerful revolutionary wisdom. It will do this if you engage in it. It's like swimming. Doing it is different than just learning about it or hoping to achieve it.

> "My experience in nature shows me that I am a person who gets good feelings when I am near or interacting with/in water. I walked to the park and found a peaceful, quiet spot near the stream. I am always attracted to water and feel a strong connection to it; I often feel a longing for being in the presence

of a body of water. I gently put my hand in the stream, allowing the current to move my fingers as if I was weaving something. It felt wonderful to relax my limb and allow the natural movement of the water to guide my thought processes. I thanked the stream for sharing the musical sounds and the cool, smooth sensations."

~Revolutionary Wisdom participant

Since I have successfully designed and continue to live, teach, and personify the revolutionary wisdom of UNE Truth for the past ninety years, you might start by trusting it and me. Then let your experience with it here be the deciding factor about applying RWE when that opportunity arises.

On these pages, I include the key components of the Truth that my students and I effectively co-mentor. If you need confidence in me, I invite you to explore my attributes and experiences (4). See <www.ecopsych.com/mjcohen.html> I have constantly lived in the 54-sense Truth of natural areas for the past sixty years.

I warranty that RWE will support *any* Truth or value you may have found or will find in 1) the demonstration 9-fact sentence in the Camera example paragraph above or 2) participant quotes. This is because *both* scientifically produced Truth that can remedy today's increasing catastrophe, the wide range of personal, social and environmental disorders that our absence of Truth produces.

Because my life was directly caught up in parts of the Catastrophe, my UNE Truth urged me to produce the Project NatureConnect Revolutionary Wisdom Expedition process **(RWE).** By applying the Truth of Climate Therapy and the Fibonacci Golden Ratio, it is a practical, evidence-based remedy for the Catastrophe's cause and symptoms. Because RWE consists of UNE Truth, it can be beneficially added to any relationship or technology. It is especially valuable to those who most suffer from or are concerned about the source of our steadily increasing maladies.

NOTE: I mark each section " All below" to further validate its facts that I later present in this book's documentary film about RWE and Climate Therapy.

PART ONE
The UNE Truth of Revolutionary Wisdom (RWE)

*In the Big Bang Unified Field, anything and everything
is attached to all that has gone before it and all that
follows it. All are always present in the Now.*
~ UNE Truth

Facts About my Integrity

 All below:

Workshop Member: *How did you first discover RWE?*

Like any and every other person, I was biologically born of, with, and as the same balanced and peaceful Truth of the life of Nature that thrives in natural areas, things and people. In me, the buried integrity of that UNE climate honesty lay abused and injured from the traumatic effects of the decapitation of my Jewish grandparent's Jewish friend during the 1900 Russian pogroms in Kiev, Ukraine.

They fled this disaster by immigrating to America, where I was brought up aware, sensitive to, and defensive of abuse to my life as a Jew, even though it was a religion, I seldom practiced. In 1938 such abuse was known in my neighborhood. I remember that people attached to Gerald L.K. Smith and Father Coughlan beat the local rabbi with a rubber hose. He got away with it since it left no bruises. I avoided these, and other menaces, by spending my time with friends in local natural areas where I loved to be. Be it a vacant lot or *forest* of towering sunflowers. A rusty trashed stove comes to mind.

When I was six, in 1936, during my first year of school, a legally required *abuse* of my left-handed biology made me uncomfortable. It was a rule that demanded I, along with everybody else, write with my right hand. My posture, speech, happiness, and family relationships deteriorated in response to that unbalancing climate. In my distress, I discovered and defended a great trustable truth of my life, I was left-handed by nature, and I was absolutely sure of that.

It took three years for my family to work out a technological solution, a fountain pen, for the school's unreasonable *writing righty* requirement. I remained acutely aware of my *lefty* truth being demeaned and I was upset in this regard. To avoid its discomfort, I designed part of my life to protect and strengthen my *great lefty Truth* whenever possible. One helpful defense was that Lefty Gomez was an all-star pitcher for the Yankees.

Other left-handers in my school classes were evidently not as sensitive to the school's right-handed intrusion of their personal nature. They did not *righteously* resist becoming righty's and no doubt capitulated to other questionable demands as well. In the process, they lost some of their natural lefty Truth. They were not as self-protective as I was about being a lefty. My being self-protective was an outcome of my family wisely being caring and careful, on-the-alert, persecuted Jewish immigrants. In hindsight, these roots help explain why I can be my RWE Truth today and scientifically assist others to do the same. Everything is attached to all that has gone before it and all that follows it.

Back then, the inkwells for our dip pens were permanently drilled into the right side of the desk. Today, left-handed desk chairs are available. Perhaps my childhood lefty-Truth and self-protection efforts helped make this balance possible.

Our Greatest Trustable Truth (GTT)

🎥 All below:

Workshop Member: *What makes the GTT so special or powerful?*

In the climate of my lefty-is-OK *crusade*, I discovered that, to their loss, most people unnecessarily suffer because they are indoctrinated to hide their Greatest Trustable Truth (GTT) from themselves by mislabeling it God, Nature, Love or Honesty. That veiling may sound unbelievable. However, ask yourself this: do you really know the greatest Truth in your life that you can trust and it is not God, Nature, Love, or Honesty? It exists. Most people don't know it because we are educated not to know it. However, and with thanks, individuals recognize it through my RWE process. In two minutes, they learn to affirm what that harmonizing Truth is and begin to put it to good use.

Our Greatest Trustable Truth (GTT) contains all of our 54 natural senses in congress, not just our limited *5-sense* stories. Limited stories seldom agree or unite with each other, so they constantly produce a climate of issues and duality. Too often, our limited 5-sense sensibility and sensitivity leave us destructively divided and wanting. Then, out of frustration or pain, we increasingly disconnect from things. However, feeling isolated and unsupported, for compensatory fulfillment, we excessively demand new things. Things are made of natural resource products and relationships accompanied by their adverse side effects. We overly seek them while ignoring that Earth's life is our life, what we do to Earth we do to ourselves. Our omission of that Truth makes the climate of the world/us fall apart from our excessive demands on our planetary life-source. It is far more than just a resource or plaything.

Believe this recovered victim, the inclusion of our absent, but easily learned, 54-sense Greatest Trustable Truth (GTT) in Industrial Society is a missing remedy to the person/planet, *Earth Misery* catastrophe we continue to create and suffer from excessively nature-disconnected management of our relationships.

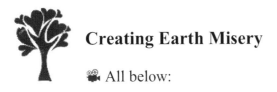

Creating Earth Misery

All below:

Workshop Member: *Is there a central problem that RWE helps us solve or is it many little ones?*

The climate of Earth Misery, since 1974, is distressful, sensed and a measurable global short circuit in our GTT-absent ability to manage, grow, and sustain balanced relationships and well-being. Bestseller books in 1948 by Fairfield Osborn and William Vogt predicted this tragic catastrophe would occur. Today, 2020, this shocking spectacle is a snowballing personal and international heartbreak, an atmosphere that results from our abusive mistreatment of the life of Nature, around, in and as us.

> *My Aboriginal grandmother married a white man in 1916. My Aboriginal father married a white girl.*
> *~ **Bronwyn Bancroft***

Aboriginals lived 30,000 years in an *"uncivilized"* balance with UNE by their stories respecting its truth. We have improved human life, but not responsibly after 1949. Via the discovery of Ecology and through bestseller books then, we knew that if we did not restrain our excessiveness, we would be out of balance. Unlike Aboriginals, we had lost conscious contact with our 54 senses in natural areas so our limited 5-sense relationships continued to be excessive even after Earth Day 1970 while we aware of the yearly increasing resource deficit statistics of 1974.

Currently, scientifically researched Earth Misery shows that, to our harm, our abuse and pain from our GTT-absent relations has produced a climate of emotional needs whose excessive fulfillment from products and substances make us produce an increasing natural resource deficit every year. To fill this balanced-living shortfall, today, we need another Planet Earth half its size to connect with our planet and replace the web-of-life *resources* that our emotional demands increasingly overuse, injure and trespass.

Be alarmed! We don't know where that missing half-planet Earth is located or how to connect with it, so we continue to increasingly live in the atmosphere of our abused and wanting lives whose daily excessiveness further deteriorates our natural-world, planetary home, including us.

An educated person knows that the life of Planet Earth is our life as well as the *natural resource* that makes our life and excessively nature-disconnected ways possible. The climate of our 45% resource deficit that is produced by our missing GTT creates a 45% increase in Earth Misery disturbances that we have suffered since 1974.

These disturbances include a destructive 45% increase in wildlife decline, mental illness, obesity, climate crisis, oceanic oxygen depletion, loneliness, atmospheric carbon, population, mass shootings, and excessive stress.

They are accompanied by increased corruption, child abuse, unhappiness, mistrust, unfairness, polarization, suicide, destructive dependencies, addiction, and many other disorders. In the past three years, life expectancy has declined rather than risen. We have started a sixth mass species extinction, and our climate crisis continues to increase.

Our unidentified, 54-sense GTT is aware of our Earth Misery atmosphere. It feels exasperated because its unifying powers know what we can do to reduce Earth Misery, and we don't do it. . Once identified and put into play, our 54-sense GTT therapeutically guides us back into balance by being added to everything we do.

"I wondered, what is my Greatest Trustable Truth I can trust in my life. Immediately I looked ahead of me, and I saw tree roots growing from a stone. This strongly touched me. The root attraction made my heart softer, and I felt rootlets slowly deep breath in my chest. It revives my inner roots. I was rooting. I watched the tree ahead of me, its roots, and its branches for a long time. In my mind, a metaphor appeared and lit my attention. '*It is like if you would like to connect with another tree with branches, but the only connecting way you should go with it is thru your roots.*' I felt safe and confident. I was/am John rooting in colorfulness, surrounded by safeness. Everything health, wise, instinctive, and intuitive is deeply rooted in me/us/it." ~ **RWE participant interaction**

All our books, teachings, and knowledge of the world since humanity began have ended up increasing Earth Misery in this moment. We are personally and collectively living out the disparaging history of our civilization's excessive, story-built relationship with the beautifully self-balanced, yet silent life of our planet. Without knowing or applying our GTT, we have nothing to use to evaluate things. Whenever we can't tell beneficial truth from destructive fiction, we can't stop acting harmfully.

Is the climate of Earth Misery believable? Do you, like many others, sense and feel it as part of your life and appreciate its antidote as our love for the Lorax, ET, Avatar, Erin Brokovich, et al.?

Time is running out! Let's get real. Space/time exists. As a boat sinks, the things in or attached to it sink with it. Because we are all living in and as our same Planet Earth *boat*, its deteriorating life is also the Earth Misery of our resource-bankrupt, deteriorating life.

We are the solitary member of the boat community that communicates and relates through stories. Being the verbal/literate part of the web-of-life, our lives are dependent on stories; the stories that spread our misleading, GTT-absent, fabrications, mistakes. Our excessiveness is sinking our planet boat and making it/us suffer accordingly. Insanity. We enjoy economic growth while bankrupt.

We have yet to admit that parts of our mentality are indoctrinated to be soldiers in the climate of *the undeclared war of our deep-state prejudice and conspiracy against the life of UNE, a life that we share and depend on.* <www.ecopsych.com/war.html>

Greatest Trustable Truth Advantages

🎥 All below:

Workshop Member: *How does RWE help us deal with Earth Misery?*

I have observed how our nature-disconnected stories and abused *inner child*, bewilderments are eviscerating the life of Earth's web-of-life, including us. Identifying and adding our absent 54-sense GTT to *God, Nature, Love, and Honesty* is the missing remedy for the atmosphere of today's devastating relationships that our omission of GTT has produced.

GTT could be said to work because the intelligence of 54-sense relationships is eleven times smarter than our limited 5-sense thinking; using 5 senses out of 54 would make our global IQ only 15 out of the average 100 IQ.

In the pages of this book, you will find the rationale, background, and opportunity to beneficially help your autobiography grow GTT relationships through the eco-arts and science of an online, 54-sense Revolutionary Wisdom Expedition. To be blunt, it invites you to win the smarter than average award for saving your planet as you save your ass. To help accomplish this, I include quotes from RWE participants, not as testimonials, but as authentic, unedited RWE journal entries that they share and co-mentor with each other online. They are from and by folks who are engaged in GTT in local natural areas via our RWE program. As participants engage in 54-sense contact and co-mentor other participants in their groups they simultaneously reduce Earth Misery. *"RWE participant interactions"* are undeniable shared journal entries. The entries demonstrate the balancing Truth that results from unadulterated, consensual, self-correcting, 54-sense GTT contacts with the natural world in authentic natural areas.

To avoid being absurd, be thankful that the participant quotes here are as GTT, as is your GTT when you disconnect from the life of Earth by holding your breath. Be assured that the suffocation pain detached-you will feel is Earth's love for you, urging you to breathe again. This is because it loves you to feed its plants the Carbon Dioxide food they deserve, that your life provides them by exhaling, as their Oxygen feeds you from their love of you and your CO_2.

🐾 Because every RWE participant is loved as a restorative, Earth Misery pioneer and patriot, our heart inherently validates and loves their contributions.

> "I was feeling anxiety pain with the crowds and trying to get outside and moving west and south to meet my friend. I thought I would try the RWE activity when I was near a park or something. However, I found that this emotional pain was a message that I needed to address ASAP! I asked for permission to be outside once I was on the sidewalk. Immediately I felt the breeze blow on my face! It was glorious, and I appreciated its consent for me to be here. It was an instant relief. I was able to breathe easier and smile. This brought me to the activity, and I thanked the breeze for bringing me back into connection. I went on a few walks with my husband this week since he took off from work. We had many discussions about nature and what I am doing. He gets why I am doing this." ~ **RWE participant interaction**

As noted, scientifically, moment-by-moment, all things are continually attached to their past and future. For this reason, the RWE participant interaction quotes here are like incidents in an Oscar-winning documentary film about how Nature works, a film produced to responsibly reduce Earth Misery. The quotes emulate and validate that the facts in this book are rooted in my extraordinary, lefty, GTT, 54 sense, RWE contacts with authentic natural areas and people (4) < www.ecopsych.com/mjcohen.html >

Extend the Director's Workshop

All below:

Workshop Member: *Is just reading about RWE helpful?*

In considering here the information I presented to the Board of Directors, it makes sense to recognize that we are looking at it with much more information about the art of my 54-sense, revolutionary expedition science than the Board Members had when their workshop commenced at the start of the 2000 millennium.

Omitted at their beginning were the understandings the preceding pages have shared. For example, they did not know, as do you now,

- the power of RWE-54 sense truths and how to learn about them through a timeless movie camera.
- what GTT actually is and the UNE reality it makes available to their investigation of the unexplained in the comparative study of religion, philosophy, and science.
- the RWE self-evidence process is GTT in action.
- my Russian pogrom family history and the valid sources I, for decades, first-hand experienced and collected in natural areas, sources that urged me to implement the RWE process.
- the existence of Earth Misery because our society, then and now, hides it from us out of shame and, in desperation, veils the influence of how it disturbs our inner child as well as our economic or social issues.
- the authenticity of all things being continually attached to their past and future and how realizing this phenomenon makes our RWE IQ 100 instead of 15.

Consider this example of how RWE helps anybody find our GTT in a natural area. It actualizes the ancient legendory Phoenix, a magnificent, mythical, long-lived bird. It would fly into a fire to be purified by flames, become reborn out of its own ashes and leap from its funeral pier into the light, resurrected, renewed and gloriously a-new.

> "There are no coincidences, a woodpecker greeted us in the forest and decaying leaves teach us about homeostasis, life and death in balance in the woods. Strangely, this cycle and the ability to maintain inner balance calmed me. It helps me leave old and unnecessary things, situations, attitudes. It reminds me of the phoenix principle. It is a perfect system where the Earth can improve itself. We often feel it ourselves. If we were to join a unified network of life, we could be much healthier. I walked to the edge of the forest at the top of the rocks, about 200 m above the river. Around there is a beautiful view of the surroundings. I immediately realized that the whole planet was creating homeostasis, otherwise we couldn't be here. I felt enormous gratitude for the Earth." ~ **RWE participant interaction**

When I was drafted into the Army they immediately trained and paid me to function in a necessary medical service they researched and offered for the public's welfare. My life became working towards all my goals plus their medical expertise skills while in the military. I creatively contributed to the global community while being paid $58/day, once a month ☺.

Today this book attests that the world is suffering from Earth Misery. It demonstrates that those in charge must be convinced to, like the military, train and pay people with RWE expertise to help stop this catastrophe by adding RWE to everything. Without its truth our Earth Misery disaster will continue to increase.

> "Your reflection made me remember an RWE exercise, years ago, next to a deep jungle/forest entrance, Our guide, an older man, did not care to participate in it and told me: "What you are sharing with these people, is what I do when I feel ill..." - "how is that?" I asked - "Well, when I feel sick, I cross the river here, and go deep in the jungle, I choose a place I feel good, and stay there, for several days and nights... I then come out and feel much better, the forest heals

me." The guide noted that his life already demonstrated the forest's healing powers." ~ **RWE participant interaction**

RWE works because as its lifelong instrument and architect, via 54-sense self-evidence, I lived and improved it for 84 years, the last 55 of them in natural areas, often on expeditions. On them, the life of Earth is also our life, I repeat, with this one noted exception: *we can speak and it can't.* However, our words too easily slide by without anchoring their 54-sense meanings in our mind, body and spirit. Here are some words along with their meanings that I've used here to honestly convey the RWE process. When you see or think of RWE, try to felt-sense it as *a blend* of these words and qualities.

- **Organic:** self-organizing, not controlled by an external agent; distributed over all relationships
- **Unite:** to come together as a single unit
- **Joy:** The emotion evoked by well-being
- **Challenge:** a query as to the proven truth of something
- **Attraction:** a force drawing things together
- **Love:** an affection for attraction
- **Revolution:** a complete change
- **Expedition:** a specific purpose journey
- **Natural:** in accordance with nature
- **Nature:** the controlling force of the Universe
- **Universe:** a whole body of things and phenomena
- **Community:** an unified body of individuals
- **Wisdom:** accumulated scientific or philosophic learning
- **Science:** evidence-based knowledge
- **Art:** the application of creative activity
- **Evidence:** Facts that support an assertion
- **Self-Evidence:** evident without proof or reasoning
- **Life:** the sequence of experiences that make up existence
- **Existence:** the state or fact of having being
- **Trust:** assured reliance on truth
- **Truth:** real things, events and fact
- **Honest:** upright and fair
- **Time:** a non-spatial continuum
- **Moment:** a minute instant
- **History:** a chronological record of events

- **Climate:** the prevailing set of conditions
- **Fiduciary:** founded in trust
- **Essence:** the ultimate nature of a thing
- **Good:** to the benefit of all
- **Therapy:** having a good effect
- **Abuse:** the mistreatment of things
- **Fair:** impartial and honest, free of prejudice
- **Legal:** established by law
  Biography: a history of a person's life

> "Thank you all for reading me, and sharing this adventure. Knowing and being one with our inner child is a relationship which many of us have lost over the years, we either feel that to offer this inner child recognition would make us somehow different in the eyes of contemporary society, such is our brainwashed state and our wish to conform to the lies we have been told in the form of rules or we have just forgotten its existence. This activity resonates with me, because my mother always placed her feelings onto me as a child, even as an older child. If she was cold, she would tell me to put on a jumper because "it was cold" whether I was cold or not made no difference to her. This is an example of when our uniqueness as individuals are clear, just because my mother was cold, does not mean that I was. Nature's diversity is such that everyone feels temperature changes differently. I innately know when I am cold and am attracted to find warmer clothing or shelter. A favorite story was the lie that if you went out in the cold with a bare neck you could catch pneumonia. I do not blame those telling lies, they have been brainwashed by society too."
> **~ RWE participant interaction**

Here's a secret that is no lie. If you value RWE's benefits you can begin to enjoy them by *reading this book aloud to an attractive natural area,* or to a pet, a plant or the sky, or to somebody's inner child. Since *Our Plundered Planet,* 1948, our excessiveness has identified us as pirates fighting over Nature as booty or loot. Be a RWE practioner instead. Love how Nature's theraputically responds in you as you read this book to it. Improve your personal climate.

Access your Greatest Trustable Truth

🎥 All below:

Workshop Member: *What's the best way for me to discover my GTT?*

Only an hour before my Spiritual Philosophy Union Director's workshop began, I thought about how I should start it. These leaders were very wise in Spiritual Philosophy and I had no formal training or experience in it. I figured what might help them was for them to know what the greatest trustable truth in their life was. This moment of thought in 2000 A.D. was the latest in my total 40 years of RWE experiences in natural areas that commenced in 1960 and continued after I left the real-time expedition. Since that question was the GTT that came to my mind in the moment, I relied on it and I began the workshop by asking its participants what I knew was true for Nature and me. I asked them, *"What is the greatest truth in your life that you can trust, and it is not God, Nature, Love, or Honesty?"*

Each Director was flabbergasted to discover that the RWE science of what made my expeditions work was also the greatest trustable truth in their life, yet they had no idea what to call it because *"God, Nature, Love or Honesty"* had hidden and replaced it. To internalize it, I had the Directors demonstrate and experience that truth's veracity for themselves.

Until that moment, without identifying it, the Directors were unaware that they could believe, trust and enjoy the GTT green light beam of logical, 54-sense information that was part of their genetic makeup as well as natural areas. They discovered that with it, they could become far more reasonable than limited, 5-sense, IQ-15 learning by using the beam's ultimate truth to authenticate information and relationships. That ray of loving, attractive fact was like a 2-way reality intensifier. Its great 54-sense certainty concretely blended into human consciousness what it simultaneously illuminated in a natural area and our body, mind, and spirit. I believe this workshop was the start of Eco-Theosophy, a nature-connected discipline that has yet to be fully established or be included in Organicism, Existentialism, Ecosophy, Anthroposophy, Objective Science, and most other ways of knowing.

> "There were still some abusive stories in my head that needed addressing. When we continue to experience nature, we continue to make the connection that we have lived in a disconnected world for so long that our nature-disconnecting stories are vast and deep. I will strive to teach others to do the same, and by allowing nature to help them in their recovery or healing processes, then they, in turn, help nature in her self-reclamation. It truly is win-win for all involved.
> **~RWE participant interaction**

Long before this workshop, my lengthy RWE quest discovered that if we don't know the GTT in our life, we can't determine or validate any other truths because we have nothing to compare other truths to. This inability is the source of most of our troubles and it confirms Confucius: "*The beginning of wisdom is to call things by their right name,*" For example, very few people seem to know that Nature is Love and Life or why the truth of mathematics works until they first know their Greatest Trustable Truth.

Here, I make available GTT to you, as I did to the Directors. Its revolutionary wisdom climate makes a critical contribution that is omitted in books, media, institutions, leaders, and contemporary life relationships. Its undeniable 54-sense accuracy is an empowering tool that we learn to take for granted and therefore ignore. I again exemplify this here and now by this special certainty: *we both know you must be reading these words right now, yet we may be differing strangers thousands of miles apart.* On some level, this is unquestionably accurate. That level is our GTT, personally and shared. It is what our 54 senses register in and as immediate moment, indisputable self-evidence. The GTT fact is that unifying multisensory experience exists in every moment and we can easily become aware of it and beneficially think, relate, and unite with it.

However obvious the italicized statement, above, may seem, it is also scientifically unexplainable in 5-sense thinking, and it fits into Albert Einstein's *"spooky action at a distance"* and *"particle entanglement"* work in Quantum physics. GTT is advanced theory and knowledge while "you are reading these words" is a reasonable, common-sense, self-evident. It is **indisputable** because it exists.

Another GTT example is if we pinch ourselves and we feel it, we know that we and our senses exist and are alive. This is also a sensory, self-evident reality. No other proof is needed. It scientifically registers and integrates directly in our existence. This singular experience is a reasonable, exact, and repeatable phenomenon for you and for anybody else, a commonly held fact of life that is more true, accurate, and valuable than 2 + 2 = 4. That is because the math equation only authentically stabilizes a specific moment while everything else, moment-by-moment, moves on and changes, including what we think and feel in and as the life of the Universe/Nature/Earth/us.

RWE is always accurate because it includes the 54 senses we inherit that register the life of our planet and us, moment-by-moment. An alert to our ego and intellect: this is no accident.

For example, think about a person writing down their GTT is as true as 2 + 2 = 4. When they then read what they wrote, it is no longer valid because what they wrote is no longer accurate. Their GTT has become that they are, what they wrote rather than writing it. Also, everything else has changed. Our GTT is what we are experiencing in the immediate moment, the truth of what our senses register exists in the moment. It is us being and knowing ourselves as a **capitalized verb:** *Being, Enjoying, Fearing, Loving, Running,* etc.

Our greatest challenge is that we consciously know our immediate moment aliveness through the truth of 54-senses, yet we learn to think that we only have five of them, our traditional *5-senses.* For this reason, you probably don't know that your sense of humor is sense number 29, or your sense of hunger is sense number 11, or your sense of place is sense numbers 30 and 34. However, you probably are aware that none of them are one of our 5-senses, touch, taste, sound, sight, and smell. Significantly, this demonstrates that the normal way we think with 5 senses out of 54. This confirms it is actually 85% less sensible than it could be. This explains a lot, especially since my *utopian* expeditions worked because we learned to RWE think and relate with 54 senses in the climate of natural areas, and anybody can easily learn to add this to what they do at home, work, or school.

> "The RWE guidebook says, 'Once we recognize discomforts from nature as being affirmative signals that guide us to overlooked attractions, we place a different image on our screen of consciousness.' This is exactly what happened when I used the anxiety feeling signal and moved to my overlooked attractions" ~ **RWE participant interaction**

What we discovered was that we inherently knew we had 54-senses, but our traditional education and society had taught us to **bury and replace** this knowledge with the same limited 5-sense information whose shortcomings make us continually produce our Earth Misery troubles. With respect to the natural world, personally or collectively, we are often abusively inaccurate, and it shows. This is not surprising once you realize we spend 99% of our lifetime disconnected from, and out-of-tune with how Nature's balanced perfection works. We are divided because our GTT is excessively estranged from the GTT of the natural world.

By helping the natural world awaken our 54-senses, my lifework produced an RWE process that enabled our groups to enjoy the self-correcting purity, balance, and beauty of Nature. This was and is a teachable climate that can be produced anywhere. Instead, sadly, it is too often taboo or omitted.

Aren't we mentally deficient? Our UNE, 54-sense, GTT/RWE has been validated and published for 35 years in eleven books and courses. Our intelligence has been indoctrinated to ignore it while our abusive Earth Misery problems that it remedies have tripled in size from what they were between 1974 to 1986.

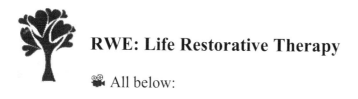

RWE: Life Restorative Therapy

🎥 All below:

Workshop Member: *Do you think that without RWE, the knowledge we now have is adequate?*

The reason that the RWE information in this book cannot continue to be omitted is our painful awareness that the climate of Earth Misery problems has become an unfathomable personal and global calamity that RWE alone can help us solve. Today, the motivation to benefit from RWE is higher for those of us who have not yet been numbed into apathy.

On our RWE internet or on-site programs, RWE folks enjoy strong fiduciary bonds to each other and to the life of our planet. We get personally and globally valid information faster and appropriately relate to it as soon as possible. For example, in 1980, our society was aware of the adverse climate effects from eating meat, and we had the means to become mostly vegetarian, yet this adjustment is still controversial today and the appropriate methods not applied. This is similarly true with respect to climate change. On an expedition quest, our strong unifying bonds as fiduciaries motivate us to expedite such things as soon as possible. In peace and joy, they responsibly RWE replace the martyrdom usually needed to make great things happen.

In RWE, a fiduciary is a person, place, or thing that holds a dedicated relationship of <u>trust</u> and confidence with the rest of RWE and acts for and on behalf of them. *Them* includes our whole planet and its life.

> "You speak to me when you say. 'When you need nature the most, it won't let you down.' I am coming to slowly realize how nature will always be there to guide us, nurture us, heal us. It really is a constant we can count on. It was neat to hear

your description of filtering through the urban jungle and sensing the natural world." ~ **RWE participant interaction**

Here I provide the profound evidence-based answers we need as well as how to immediately apply them by engaging in RWE to the extent that each individual's thinking permits. It is the engagement that makes RWE work. This is just like our survival lies in the realization that we don't eat a dollar bill, that, instead, we use it to buy food; the act of eating food, not money, sustains our life energy.

To help you benefit from RWE, its origins, rationale, results, and values tell their story here. They convey my experiences as RWE's founder as well as the authenticity of its participants' involvement, the same GTT information, now updated, that was produced and beneficially experienced during the Board of Directors workshop in 2000 AD.

As a reminder, to make the great Truth of RWE less foreboding, included here is information as it has been recorded in RWE Field Journaling. The shared quotes are from *emails to each other* of online, RWE participants as they actualize, co-create, and co-mentor RWE in a natural area moment, backyard or back country. They share with their groups something like a scientifically spiritual or sacred RWE experience, a repeatable GTT harmonic reality that helps them reverse the climate of Earth Misery.

> "When asking a natural area, I was attracted to, and then gaining permission to visit it, I asked the question, "How many children should I have?" The resulting GTT story I told myself was "NONE!" This was based on the Earth Misery experience I had of being abused by others and also abusing others, protecting others being abused (yes co-dependent here!) and addictively tranquilizing the pain through alcohol, and through worrying about my heroin-addicted daughter, and so busily taking my spouse's inventory incessantly."
> ~**RWE participant interaction**

If it helps you, think about how most social media posts could be similar to the shared posts here and what the world might be like then. If, instead, you want to learn to do this by 54-sense being it, here's your *dollar* to, free of charge, engage in RWE (26): visit www.ecopsych.com/LNE.html. You can spend it anytime and bring RWE into your life, and vice-versa.

> "Heather, I enjoy these online RWE visits. I am transported to your Now through sensory labeling, language description, and digital photography in nature's wonderfully nurturing, authentic swamp. Thank you for sharing these moments in such vivid detailing. We often refer to it being '*triggered*' in a negative frame. I am triggered in the most delightful ways through your expression. Your healing space transcends proximity and time. Sending much love." ~ **RWE participant interaction**

We are super-intelligent and powerful, in a good way, when our thoughts and relationships produce a therapeutic climate of RWE stories that eliminate the things that separate us and offset their destructive effects. We desperately need this RWE unifying force today. It holds all things together. It is the very unity that we seek while we ignore it. Its absence has us increasingly dis-integrating rather than uniting through natural, 54-sense love.

> *A nature negative is a **receptive attraction** which continually signals and protects us. Receptive attractions guide us to connect with our innermost self so we can attain a state of homeostasis.*
> ~ *Stacey S. Mallory*

"One of the joys of finding RWE is the fact that the philosophy that Mike has developed over time is not just one person's way of thinking, but a way of thinking that is inherent in all living things. It is a matter of digging deep and allowing that way of thinking to resurface. RWE gives us the opportunity to explore and evolve in this process. As a scientist, I was immediately drawn to it after reading about the evidence behind 54-sense validation. RWE discusses and involves us in the Big Bang and how it is connected to the origins of humanity. Some people do not believe in science, let alone Big Bang facts. I think that those folks are missing out on the greatest gifts God or spirit has ever given us, the ability to precisely use our minds and think about who we are, where we came from, and our purpose on this planet." ~ **RWE participant interaction**

RWE easily explains this marvel as it engages you in the balancing essentials I present here. It gives you the extraordinary ability to increase well-being by your reliable GTT scientifically, building unified, beneficial relationships on every level.

"Here I am, in beautiful Colorado, working and learning amongst 20 other individuals to become a Wilderness Therapy Guide. This practice focuses mainly on the senses and how to experience nature with those senses. I find myself being judgmental at times, feeling as though the practice is so basic compared to the RWE ways in which we have been asked to explore our 54 senses, week in and week out, pushing my boundaries to "feel" more "see" more "experience" more. All in all, however, it has been so healing to be surrounded by like-minded souls." ~ **RWE participant interaction**

RWE and Earth Misery

🎥 All below:

Workshop Member: *Do you have additional books that can help me apply my GTT?*

Revolutionary Wisdom: How to Increase Well-Being with Your 54-sense Natural Intelligence is a workbook, co-authored by Dr. Stacey Mallory and myself. It, along with my white paper application, *How to Liberate Your Natural Essence, the Art and Science of Sensory Validation* enables you to understand and make RWE happen as an added dimension to an individual or group in a local area, online, or on a global internet expedition.

These two books crystalize the eleven other books I have written. They became valid for all people when I knew that I had finally learned how to register and speak GTT for a natural area. I knew how to do this because I had unknowingly first learned to do it with members of my Columbia University Teacher's College doctoral counseling therapy courses. In those groups, you had to first gain consent or permission from a person you wanted to interact with. Otherwise, you might unknowingly be trespassing or abusing parts of them that had already been abused, sometimes known as *hooking* these feelings or *pushing their buttons*. That created problems rather than helped folks solve them together. In the courses, consciously gaining permission to visit and interact with each other solved this challenge for all parties who dedicated themselves to co-creating a safe time and space for this to happen (thank you Dr. Goodwin Watson). I simply applied this same agreement to any natural area I was attracted to visit. I first gained its consent to visit it.

"The RWE training book asks 'If you take into account today's unsolved problems that are obliterating the natural world, and you visit a natural area, and it could speak, what might the life of nature and earth sense, feel or convey about you visiting it?' I know it would sense fear and distrust me due to humanity's invasive Earth Misery destructiveness. I don't think I'd be welcome. I think this is why I see animals flee or hide when I approach but not when other animals get near them."
~ **RWE participant interaction**

 **How to Gain Consent**

🐾 All below:

Workshop Member: *Is there a key thing or activity that can help me find my GTT in a natural area?*

Below is how and why you make your GTT in RWE work.

The complete text, procedures, and outcomes are available at (29) <www.ecopsych.com/amental.html.>

Follow the instructions below written in **bold** and consider their explanations.

1. Nature enables things to build balanced and pure relationships through natural attraction energies. **Notice how you feel right now, then go to something in nature that you like that you find attractive.** A park, backyard, aquarium, even a pet or potted plant will do. Their attractiveness is the tangible sensory connection of some of our 54 natural senses being activated in the moment. That love invites, welcomes, and consciously, feelingly connects you to them. Just like thirst naturally attracts you to water, or contact with water may make you thirsty, you are biologically built to naturally connect with the Earth community through cohesive sensations; natural loves that can't tell stories but feel good. Note that thirst is not one of your *five senses*. The more natural and attractive a natural area or thing is, the more beneficial are the results of this activity. A goldfish or a flower may be better than a wilderness area if it is more attractive to you.

2. **Thank the Greatest Trustable Truth (GTT), natural attraction, that brings you to this area for being there for you**. It exists at that moment. Thank it for safely activating a good feeling in you through this attraction connection.

3. Recognize that as part of the life of Earth community, justifiably, as is true in your life, this natural area or thing desires and has a right to exist, enjoy beneficial relationships and grow, just as you do. As you may discover, in scientific reality, over the eons, Nature's attractions have loved you into being. **Decide that you are going to respect its natural integrity** by asking for permission to visit it.

4. Because our story way of life socializes us to think and act in nature-disconnected or excessive nature-conquering ways, we are foreigners to the life of this area. We build relationships through stories, accurate or not, that it doesn't understand, and this, too, often rejects or harms it.

Silently, aloud or in writing, **respectfully ask this natural area for its consent for you be there and do this activity with it there.** It will not give you permission to visit if you are going to injure, destroy or defame it, or if it will not be safe for you because negative relationships are not attractive. **Promise this area that you will treat it honorably because you love your life (to survive), and your life is also Earth's life and vice versa.**

5. **Sense the area for seven seconds or more in silence and respect**. Be aware of negative signals from stress, discouragement, or danger from it, such as thorns, bees, poison ivy, ticks, cliff faces, or unpleasant memories, thoughts, or feelings. If they appear, thank them for their *attractive* message to help you more safely find more attractive ways to obtain reasonably good feelings and rewards.

FOR EXAMPLE: "Our group was asked to select something attractive, sight unseen, from a bag full of miscellaneous objects. One adult woman blindly selected a piece of wood in the bag because she was attracted to its shape and smoothness when she groped and explored it by touch. But she had a negative reaction to the wood once she took it out of the bag and saw it. At first, she did not know why she didn't like it when she viewed it, but in time, perhaps through her dreams, she realized it was a subconscious reaction. The wood was the same shade of blue as the walls of a room where, as a child, she had been molested. Ordinarily, during the 7 second waiting period, another attraction would have appeared for her if she could have seen the painted color of the stick."

A. When the seven seconds are up, **note that if the area still feels attractive, or has become more attractive.** If either happens, GTT has consented to your visit through a multitude of your 54 natural senses (6).

See Appendix A or www.ecopsych.com/insight53senses.html

B. If you do gain consent, proceed to 6.

B-2. If this part of the natural area no longer feels attractive or is replaced by another attraction, thank that GTT for its guidance and simply select another natural part of the area that feels attractive to you. Then repeat the gaining permission process. **Do this until you find a seven second GTT period when a safe attraction feeling remains for a place, color, shape, sound, or other natural things.** When this occurs, you have multisensory permission to visit it. In that safe GTT moment, many additional natural senses are happily connecting and consenting, too.

6. As soon as you gain a natural attraction's permission to visit, **genuinely thank it for giving its consent.**

7. Now: **Compare how you feel about being in this mutually supportive natural area moment with how you felt when you first started doing this activity.** Has any change occurred because you GTT gained the life of this area's consent and thanked it for consenting? Does the area feel better or friendlier to you? Do you find it or yourself more attractive, ethical, or rewarding now than before you received its consent and thanked it? Do you GTT feel better about yourself, more supported by the global life community? Do you feel less stressed or depressed?

Is the natural area safer because your love for it has increased, and we best protect what we love?

7-A. Write down what occurred, and if you obtained good feelings or rewards from doing this activity, what they were and whether you trust them. See if you can identify which of you 54 natural senses were involved (6).

See Appendix A or www.ecopsych.com/insight53senses.html.) **Share this information with people close to you or others who are doing the activity.**

If you find that thankfully gaining permission to visit the unifying life of a natural area GTT is rewarding, **remember that whenever you want to feel rewardingly balanced, less stressed or greater happiness, you can repeat this RWE activity and create a better climate for yourself and Earth.**

The activity's secret unifying power is that its permission in words makes safe space for harmonic, 54-sense natural attractions, around us and within us, to bridge the gap that our words usually produce because they are foreign or hostile to the natural world's seamless, yet wordless, unity. This is like being given $1000 if we hold our breath for 3 minutes, so we do it. As already mentioned, during this period, we deny plant life's attraction to have us inhale their oxygen so they can help us stay alive while they gather carbon-dioxide from us that we are attracted to exhale and help them stay alive.

For a minute as we hold our breath, life stands still until we are attracted to produce reasonable words and/or feelings. They tell/motivate us to breathe after thirty seconds and live, so we respire (inspire and expire, spire, meaning *spirit*). It is our reasonable, unifying GTT story and desire to live that permits us to breathe again and benefit plant life and our life. Otherwise, we end up transformed into other attractive parts of Nature as well as without $1000 for our headstone.

"I first seek permission to carry out this activity so that I may learn from Mother Earth's teaching and guidance. After a short time in this natural area, I am treated to a welcome by nature, trashing my technological thinking and, moment-by-moment, attracting me to its attractiveness. After gaining consent, I immediately felt GTT "now" in the balance of nature, as reflected in my own balance in the present moment. Strengthened by my senses of hearing the birds, cicadas, hawks, a feeling of peace and calmness came to me via my connection to my nervous system through earth's nervous system. The original rupture that attracted me to do this activity was my feelings of isolation and some loneliness after being sick with a cold and my spouse away for the weekend. The GTT nurturing I felt-sensed in the now was a comfort to me. Asking for and waiting to gain consent is so crucial to healing. Seeking permission is a huge piece of the puzzle of connection, especially in the current relationships between human to human as well as with nature."

~ RWE workshop email

As demonstrated above, my RWE process at Project NatureConnect is a social technology, an organic tool that lets us remedy what ails us. Without applying this Applied Ecopsychology GTT know-how organically, we continue to increasingly create the catastrophic personal, social, and environmental Earth Misery disasters that we now suffer.

My *Gain Consent* activity was done on Earth Day 1970, which preceded Earth Misery day (Earth Overshoot Day) by four years. However, by 1980, it was evident that we immediately needed to "Personally Think and **Act *Globally,***" in addition to acting ***locally***. Online, or on-site, RWE makes this possible by helping folks learn, actualize, and teach their balancing GTT in natural areas because it is universal and interspecies and can be added to most things.

 **GTT in the Now**

All below:

Workshop Member: *Is there a fundamental, evidence-based element that makes my GTT work?*

Amongst educated people, since 1925, it is a commonly accepted scientific fact that the life of our Universe grows its own time and space, moment by moment. It and we only exist in each present instant, the now moments that exist before even your essence can think or say anything. As part of the now, we and the rest of the web-of-life are loved into, result from, and are attached to this instant. Obviously, it exists. It is all of the life of the Universe that has gone before us that loves to be present and survive, moment-by-moment, now, as it seamlessly becomes all the additional time and space moments that it loves to grow for itself. **It is us; we are it because <u>all are one essence in the moment</u>.** This is the source of our GTT.

RWE can be seen as an actualization of Environmental Arts, Environmental Education, and Eco-Existential Positive Psychology. It makes finding one's GTT in a natural area the core of Pantheism and Eco-Existentialism, a philosophy RWE is inventing to help some folks be sure that Nature exists and is alive.

> "What else can I say as I read your message and tears of joy and realization gather in the corner of my eyes? 'Love, thy magic spell is everywhere.' Beautifully you merge your father's words into the feelings and senses of NOW! Part of what RWE has taught me is that we often disregard love in some respects by making it an exception to our reality "magic" when it is as natural as life itself. Your nature-connection naturalized love for me as I read it. It is the same realization that dawns on me periodically and reminds me of how human love really looks when it is natural and honest, and we are too!" ~ **RWE participant interaction**

Each space/time moment of our planet's life is the continued growth of the life of the Universe since its birth, the Big Bang beginning of time and space 13.8 billion years ago to now. For example, each now moment includes the beginning of this sentence, you are reading to this period. This is the space/time *Fibonacci Golden Ratio* in action.

What evidence-based measurements show is that from 1974 until now, person/planet Earth Misery deterioration has been increasing. This fact comes from the science of Earth Overshoot Day. The latter painstakingly establishes which day of each year the life of our Planet runs out of the resources that it needs to survive for that year. Earth's life ran out of the resources and integrity it needed to live in balance on December 30. A few years later, it ran out December 25, 4 days earlier, and this stress-inducing Earth Misery trend has continued yearly. This year, 45 years later, our planet ran out of the ability to sustain its life five months earlier, on July 29, 2019. We seldom hear the GTT that the life of Earth, and us, are increasingly stressed, bankrupt, and at risk due to our abusive, need-fulfillment excessiveness.

> "Ann, what I find most attractive is the wisdom behind your natural area attractions. To me, it seems the nesting of the bird you observed, the delicate balance of just enough, triggered you to begin the healing of a collective human breach of "not enough," which I find drives our consumerism. I do hope you continue to find sanctuary in nesting wisdom."
> **~ RWE participant interaction**

It is far beyond a reasonable doubt that we must engage in internet and on-site, evidence-based, revolutionary counseling and education expeditions that expertly teach and apply the GTT equilibrium of our RWE 54-sense antidote as an organic *App* of Ecopsychology and everything else.

My GTT

🎥 All below:

Workshop Member: *What do you think makes you competent to have created and teach RWE?*

As I describe my life on my personal page (4), I believe I am more qualified than most to know whereof, I speak about our relationship with Nature. My pages here are an overview of my heartfelt 84 years of natural area life science experience and professional training along with my programs and books for combatting our abuse of the life of our person and planet. For this personal commitment, I have been dubbed a maverick genius (32), a reincarnation of Henry David Thoreau and "in the woods too long," the latter since I unashamedly love the life of our planet and know myself as a personification of its Unified Field.

I only respect relationships that include the GTT of 54 senses in an authentic natural area. Only there can we genuinely blend with the fact that *Natural attraction (love) is conscious of what it is attracted to (loves)* (28). That loving fundamental has wisely organized itself and acted accordingly since the beginning of time, if not before, to this instant and attraction is the essence of love. This organic Applied Ecopsychology truth is the core of Experiential Education in natural areas. It can beneficially be added to any experience and increase balance, in and around us, by reducing excessiveness.

That my RWE nature-reattachment process or tool uniquely reduces Earth Misery has yet to be scientifically disputed. To our loss, however, at this late date, RWE has yet to be appropriately acknowledged no less applied to the total knowledge and relationships of society today. The excessiveness of our indoor world ego, academics, and arrogance too often dismiss natural area wisdom as inappropriately primitive.

Because the life of Earth is in a deteriorating state, sadly, moment-by-moment, no matter how much we improve our personal, environmental, and social relationships, it seldom diminishes the fundamental, point source cause of Earth Misery, so its climate continues to grow. This means that now, already bankrupt and in deficit, we increase it whenever we don't include its nature-reconnecting RWE remedy in our thinking and relationships. That indicates that some person, place, or thing unnecessarily suffers accordingly, including us and ours. This is bad personal and planetary karma, and, moment-by-moment, RWE is its remedy.

"I think RWE as a whole is more than helpful in dealing with any form of abuse or corruption, especially because it helps us live in now-moment GTT, reminding us that it is the only time that really exists. (in fact, the now-moment is not part of linear time, it exists in and as eternity). When we 54-sense experience ourselves and the world in the now, things unify. Past negative experiences and stories lose some of their strength and become less painful, so they can be approached from a different perspective. Through RWE, we tap into the 'speechless eons of unconditional love that is attracted to all and excludes nothing.' And love is the most powerful healing energy in this universe. As we heal, we experience more happiness, which in turn increases our integrity, and this brings about a climate of more happiness and more healing, establishing a virtuous circle of healing, happiness, and growth." ~ **RWE participant interaction**

Our Core Disorder

All below:

Workshop Member: *What is the major challenge we face in adding RWE to our lives whenever possible?*

We must **stop our denial**! Together, our head and heart know it is immoral, unethical, and insane for us to continue to increase our climate of personal, social, and global corrosion. This is especially true since ending it is RWE doable and *dirt* cheap. Just becoming aware of our idiocy by itself is disturbing. It usually increases our imbalance and stress, and that adds to Earth Misery. This is a vicious circle that makes us ignore this irritating fact, shrug our shoulders, and live in further disconnected numbness.

By 1980 the increase in Earth Misery was known, and many socially and environmentally responsible processes and technologies that could reverse it were available then, as they are today. Why have we not used them with thanks? Expressed with appropriate disdain, the reason is that *We don't know Jack.* That *Jack* is Jack Schitt and his Earth Misery family members (Holie Schitt along with Fulla, Dohngiva, Loda, Pounda, Hoarse, Bull, Stewpad, and the twins: Deep and Dip Schitt.) Here is why we are miserably up Schitt's Creek without a paddle.

> Jack Schitt bought a power drill to fix his boat and accidentally drilled a hole through its floor. As water gushed in, he drilled another hole in the floor to let the water out.
>
> As the water quickly rose, Jack yelled for help, and a scientist passing by repeatedly called, *"Plug up the holes!"* but to no avail. Even though he could plug the holes, Jack, instead, drilled additional holes.

We are all with Jack in the Box, his Earth Misery box, and things are not making sense. Deafness, different language, background noise, PTSD, imbalance etc. may have interfered with the solution offered by the scientist to help Jack. Maybe it was from Jack having been abused or a disorder in his mentality. He wanted to stop the boat from sinking, but he could not respond appropriately.

That global madness of Jack/Us is intolerable, and it must be treated accordingly. It insanely supports rather than reverses Earth Misery, and we are running out of time to confront Jack and let RWE refocus his behavior. RWE gets Jack's mind out of the limits of his boat, the *Houseboat that Jack built.*

> "I walked kind of numb toward my natural area spot feeling run over by the stress all around, of late. Maybe there is a resonance with the malaise of this day that years ago blackened the world; maybe it's just my black mood. Plop, I go to the ground, and instantly she receives me. Cradling me like a mother. I am her child. The earth's child. I want to show up and do my part with this RWE group, so I push down the resistance and ask about me having children. The answer comes like an IMAX movie, brilliant and textured. I am a mother and a child, a sister, aunt, and friend. My genealogy is earth. From earth, I come, and it is that earth I bear. We are all one. The answer is there is peace, and this is where I think I'll stay - for now. The fact most with me is we live IN, not on, the life of planet Earth, as fiduciaries of it and each other."
> **~ RWE participant interaction**

SOS! While the health of our vessel and us is sinking and although these RWE reasons and their solution have been available for 40 years, we still don't use them and suffer because we don't know Jack, and we remain boxed in his house. It has yet to be recognized as *The box that we want to think outside of*, the story-closet that removes our 54-sense GTT from our natural area awareness, so we further abuse the natural world around and as us.

Many people think we can safely continue to increase economic growth and development while they are fully aware that the Earth Misery life of our planet is already harmfully out of balance and bankrupt. This demonstrates that they don't know Jack.

We say our problems exist because we are greedy. What this really means is that, unlike other non-story members of the Web-of-Life community, our nature-disconnecting stories stress us, so we lose sight of physical and emotional satisfaction we may enjoy from our 54 sensory roots in the natural area life of our planet. To our loss, we gain fulfillments from questionable artifacts and imbalanced, nature-estranged human love instead.

The absence of our organic natural world satisfactions makes us excessively want, so we feel there is never enough. That defines greed. We need more of everything, we profit from things we sell to reduce our organic love deficit. We are not given a solution for this runaway wanting and greed disorder, so we believe there is no way we can fix it.

We suffer because, along with Jack in his box, we don't respond to the RWE means offered by "*some foreign, scientific passerby.*" Deep inside, we know that our greedy deterioration of the life of Earth and us are ethical, moral, and economic idiocy. This also disturbs us further and adds to our distress, so we become greedier and need more.

My description of Jack and us is a little different than the 2 percent of adult Americans who are firmly convinced Earth is as flat as a pancake. 41% of us believe humans existed with dinosaurs even when shown proof that we missed each other by 67 million years. 31% of American adults say they believe in ghosts, while in 1978, just 11% of the public believed in them. 80% believe in angels, while 90% don't know that there is scientific consensus on climate change.

Some people probably believe that a terrorist actually burnt his lips on the exhaust pipe of a bus he was trying to blow up.

"Bill, if this helps, I add '*ness*' and '*ing*' to knowing me and a natural area as an in-common verb and essence, so our words and natural balance unify. 'Ness' is 'ess'ence and 'ing' makes things a verb, an action, be-ing. I am Lee. To be my natural essence, I am Leeness. As Don's email has helped me understand, when I engage in 54-sense unifying with a natural area, my essence, my Lee-ness energetically extends outward for permission to engage. If attractions, such as my senses of beauty, community, and trust, seem open and pleasant with an Oak tree, Leeness continues to energetically engage and continue with Oakness in the moment. That's what our essence-in-common loves to do. When attractions are lasting, Leeness then merges the attraction, for example, my attraction to an Oak tree would also be a verb, too, Leeing with Oaking or Leenessing with Oaknessing. This births a new me, one with the conscious love to merge in the moment with Oaknessing in my GTT experience. This is equally true, by consent with people, out of habit, Leenessing with Bettynessing. USAnessing can merge with Russianessing, too." ~ **RWE participant interaction**

Two basic explanations for our ignorance and greed are possible. They pertain to Jack and to the RWE means to fix the problems we face on our worldwide Earth Misery boat in distress.

One questionable explanation for Jack's folly is that he was *absurd* or *stupid,* meaning that although he was aware of other sensible things, he did not use them, and *"You can't cure stupidity."* Actually, you can sometimes revive deadened senses if you apply RWE. Its 54-sense thinking and relating process improve things 108% as it augments, counteracts, or replaces our abused or numbed 54-sense ability to reason. Until then, Jack remains dumber than slime mold.

Slime molds, possibly the original one-celled, land-based form of life, go back almost a billion years, yet they redefine what we need to qualify as intelligent. They carefully explore their environments, seek the most efficient routes between resources, including the layout of man-made transportation networks, and choose the healthiest food from a diverse menu—and all this without a brain or nervous system, and we contain their genetics as part of ours. [1]

The other explanation is that Jack was *prejudiced* against the passerby, or against stopping the flow of water or against authority or who knows what may have annoyed him. His mentality rejected the obvious benefits that the scientific passerby's solution contributed. If Jack, in reality, purposely intended to collect on the boat's insurance, couldn't that be prejudice against honesty?

Prejudice is an irrational alienation whose attachments prevent reasonable responses in a reasonable amount of time. It omits the world's sense of Reason (Sense #42). The cure for prejudice is familiarity, from being attracted by 54 natural senses, not just 5, to rewarding RWE relationships that transform our prejudicial alienation back into our nature-connected love of life in people, places, and things.

August 6, 2007: Researchers[2] gave a group of 3-5-year-old children, two identical servings of many different kinds of food. The only difference between the two servings was that one was wrapped in a McDonald's wrapper, the other in a plain wrapper. Overwhelmingly, the children said the food placed in the McDonalds wrapper tasted better. Their natural self was *misled*. Their senses and sensibilities had been prejudicially brainwashed by the *story* on the wrapper before they were age six.

> "The breach that made this RWE a valuable healing experience is that part of me that still needs to heal, around my own feelings about myself and about my daughter. Also, feeling that lost child in me that still gets scared at times of uncertainty." ~ **RWE participant interaction**

At my workshop, I gave the Directors the following example of prejudice to help them understand the origins of our prejudice

---

[1] https://www.nytimes.com/2011/10/04/science/04slime.html
[2] http://abcnews.go.com/Health/Healthday/Story?id=4508191&page=3

against nature and the hurtful effects of our unbalanced relationship with our planet.

On our 1977 school year of the expedition, we visited the controversial Leaky prehistoric archeology site in Calico, California. Here were the remains of stone axes allegedly chipped out by stone-age people more than 20,000 years ago. The archeologist showed us how to make stone axes in their ancient way, using rocks as hammers to cut and chip the stone. The students used rocks as hammers all morning and successfully made several axes. We then proceeded to Death Valley, arriving in a blinding dust storm. We immediately began to set up our tents on extremely hard clay soil, so hard that we could neither hand-push nor foot-stomp our tent pegs in as we normally did.

It surprised me to find all but three of the students standing in line, coughing, with eyes tearing, all waiting to use our one single geology hammer to hammer in their tent stakes. Only three of us were not in line. We already hammered in our stakes using rocks that were in plain sight on the ground all around us.

The inconceivable had happened. Eighteen teenagers and adults who had been directed and taught to use rocks for hammers just three hours before had somehow forgotten that rocks could be used as hammers. Choking, with windblown sand stinging their face and eyes, they waited in line for their turn to use the one, manufactured, metal, available geology hammer. This was the prejudice of attached, habitual thinking and relationships in action. Several participants complained that the school was irresponsible, that many more *store-bought* hammers should have been available for situations like this.

Most references to *prejudice against nature* on the search engines link to my 1982 book on the subject, or to my web pages and articles about it. There are still no global or local searches for this prejudice. Most of us don't even believe nature is alive. That injures us and produces Earth Misery because, again, Nature's life is our life, as I demonstrate in later pages here or see (9) <www.ecopsych.com/livingplanetearthkey.html.>

We are disturbed because our nature-disconnected stories disturb or deaden us, and we don't use 54-sense RWE to remedy this malady while in a natural area. How different is this than the drunk who lost his watch one night in the middle of a city block and never found it because he *reasonably* searched for it at the street corner where the light was much brighter?

We can't afford to ignore the heartfelt RWE tool that unjust stupid or prejudicial education, counseling, and healing omits, and thereby indoctrinates us to omit in our daily lives. Your challenge is that if you do not apply this 54-sense truth, it won't work or make sense until you do. Fortunately, doing this is easy, you are doing it now. Its irrefutable veracity here, again, is that *you are reading these words, and I and others know it.* If you recognize this as an undeniable fact, you are not prejudiced in this regard, and in a local garden or park, RWE participation strengthens your GTT reasonableness in 54 ways. You can easily apply this same dependable *now* truth to all things by using the RWE process, a natural area power tool that empowers you to apply it.

> "Ruth, thank you for sharing your butterfly experience! What a long trip you have made, with detailed, thoughtful preparation in so many respects! What strikes me is the depth - of your connection, and thanks to what you describe as the "deep throbbing pulse of the Earth Mother." How this force and power penetrates to your core-- again, the penetration, the Essence. All else, the songs, the hums, the croaks, the drifts, the motions come out of this. Gratitude is such a natural response, isn't it?" ~ **RWE participant interaction**

In summary, Earth Misery is the problem on our planetary boat that our Society's ignorance about the natural world, and prejudice against Nature prevents us from solving at this late date. As today's troubles show, these phenomena also prevent us from creating advanced scientific contact and 54-sense heightened balanced connections that remedy these two areas. For example, my local grant organization refused to fund RWE teacher training. They said they did not work with *religious cults.*

Folks make the time and funds available to fly to some far-away place and visit some practitioner of a foreign, ancient culture to help them deal with today's high-tech Earth Misery. They could, instead, accomplish this locally, without adverse air-traffic impacts, via counseling that included RWE and Environmental Art in their backyard and use the money saved to help others do the same. That would decrease rather than increase Earth Misery.

The antidote for prejudicial stories is RWE space and time for deeper attractions, and 54-sense love to be energized into action.

> "It is Sunday, and even here, in my wilderness retreat, I have a long list of things to do. But, for now, I am sitting peacefully, taking in my surroundings, and reveling in my being. I am remembering why I make the trek, why I am so strongly drawn to this place. Here, more than any other, I deeply sense and feel the aliveness, the deep throbbing pulse of my, our, Mother! This energy, the force, and power of life penetrates to the marrow of my bone. The soft whispers of the breeze in the fir trees; the cacophony of birds songs; the hum of the hummingbirds in flight; the croak of the ravens; the gentle drift of the clouds; the strength and durability of the mountain; the perpetual motion of the river; and, perhaps mostly, the absence of the energy, noise, and desperation of human endeavor. All of this ignites my senses, my awareness of being alive, in this moment, in this place! I feel profoundly grateful for this gift, the opportunity to walk, breathe, and participate in this beautiful Mystery, in this magnificent planet!"
> **~RWE participant interaction**

The Key: Invoke RWE Organic Guidance

📽 All below:

Workshop Member: *Is there any single example that that best helps people understand RWE?*

My white paper, *How to Liberate Your Natural Senses*, empowers folks, including Jack, to use and teach RWE by addressing the challenge in the following scenario.

We suffer our problems because, in metaphor, the story of Industrial Society has, for our comfort, emotionally attached us to drive an advanced technology automobile. As we excessively speed this vehicle down the highway to relieve our stress or distress, or for fun, or late for an appointment panic, we are alarmed to see that the car, suddenly uncontrolled, will go into a group of families having an RWE training workshop and picnic in a beautiful natural area.

Because we have not yet troubled ourselves to learn how to fully activate the car's optional organic braking and steering system, in anguish we hope and pray that the vehicle will stop as we fearfully scream *"Oh God,"* or *"Whoa"* or *"STOP"* like the vehicle was an evil spirit or a runaway horse, or that it understood words and feelings.

The reactions above are unscientific, outdated, and don't work. They do not help Jack stop our high-tech car, so we wreak Earth Misery havoc on people, places, and things, including us as passengers. We are guilty and must be punished for DUI, Driving Under Ignorance. **Scientifically, how could this not be so? How can we realistically stop the car and help Jack, too?**

What we need to apply is the car's RWE organic science and technology brake and guidance, It is a great truth that helps us register and apply the wise, self-correcting, ways that are inherent in the life of a slime mold, a natural area and us. We would then know and apply the natural world's organic intelligence, balance, and purifying powers that have protected and preserved its/our life over the eons. That 54-sense truth would help us wisely manage the car. Its absence is the Jack in the box that lets our car and us continue to create Earth Misery. To not stop it via RWE organics is our lie or sin of omission as we become immoral criminals in our undeclared war against Nature (39) <www.ecopsych.com/war.html>

✤ All below:

Jack, listen up! The brake guide and RWE only work if you apply them. Happily, fill the holes in your life and your boat reasonably. Learn to use RWE by helping that well-intentioned scientist learn it.

> "I sometimes need my mom too, Kathy. The morning after her death (which I was by her side for), a mourning dove appeared in my back yard for the first time. The cooing, calming, and presence of her was as a great validation as I could receive of the mystery that life goes on in ways beyond what any of us have storied and worshiped yet. Nature knows. I will let her keep teaching me into the homeostatic presence of ever balancing love." ~ **RWE participant interaction**

How to employ the RWE brake is relatively simple for us to learn since, as part of Nature, we have genetically inherited, sense, and register this information. We just have to know how to put it into words and with them create a scientifically accurate guidance system story, our RWE 54-sense, 24-fact brake social technology. This organic management tool reasonably unifies and motivates our senses, feelings, and relationships. **Is it wise, moral, ethical, or legal to omit it? Would its exclusion stand up to a class action suit against withholding a remedy for our constitutional right to life that is free of stress disorders, mental illness, climate crisis, pollution, and species loss, to life both mentally and environmentally healthy? (25)**

> "I stop taking steps and look down – see an ant, carrying a small piece of a leaf – headed somewhere intently. I feel a sense of belonging here (#34, sense of emotional place, of

community, belonging, support, trust, and thankfulness, #35, sense of self including friendship, companionship, and power). While everything is going about its business, it is holding space for me. A sense of support and love exists here (#40, sense of humility, appreciation, ethics), and that I am a part of this whole aliveness (#52, sense of survival by joining a more established organism, #54, the self-evident, unifying, love of love sense of natural attraction as the singular mother essence and source of all other senses)."
~ **RWE participant interaction**

"In this Now moment – I can see movement – everything is in constant movement. Absolutely nothing is still, yet even in the movement, there is calmness, and I don't feel chaos (#49, relaxation, and sleep). Yet when I am at home or other human settings, the more movement there is, the more chaos I feel. I am awe-struck at how nature balances movement and calmness simultaneously (#53, spiritual sense, including conscience, the capacity of sublime love). I am grateful for this (#34, sense of emotional place, of community, belonging, support, trust, and thankfulness.)"
~ **RWE participant interaction**

Similar to us not reducing our stress disorders, the Directors at the workshop did not continue with RWE, so Earth Misery increased. This omission did not have the visibility or impact of 911 because people's lives were not lost, or a bumper sticker or high-tech *app* was not available.

Along with the stunned Directors and Jack, for you to believe and act like the car's 54-sense brake works, you must understand, trust and love how and why it does. To this end, consider just one of our 54 senses, our sense of thirst. Note again that it is not included as one of today's five-senses that *Jack* Aristotle identified in 350 B.C. Note that his awareness, along with that of everybody else back then, did not know how to screw in a light bulb. That was invented in 1879 A.D.

Thirst is more than just a sensation or sense (#21). It is also a wisdom that, in the moment, for our increased comfort and survival, it makes us connect with the global water cycle and bring its water into and through us to replace the water we have lost as well as to cleanse us. Thirst is also a balancing global intelligence. It is smart enough to turn on when it knows that we need water and to turn off when we have enough. Then our sense of excretion continues, and we give the planet the perfect food and water that its life needs.

Similarly, our sense of respiration does the same with CO_2 and H_2O. Stop breathing, and its suffocation discomfort tells you to start. This *synchronicity* is an RWE absolute.

As exemplified by thirst, on cellular and molecular levels, sensors (senses and their sensations) in an organism, large (Earth) or small (nanobe), are receptors that are attracted to detect stimuli. When the information that they register is out of balance, they become the main homeostatic driving force for change that promotes life in balance. Their detection process is a fundamental attraction source that functions on mechanical, thermal, and chemical levels as it loves to promote the survival of life. When they are not adulterated by nature-disconnected stories, the senses can be depended on as self-evident, recovery and balancing tools that are part of every space/time moment. Whatever any of our 54 senses find attractive in Nature is what in Nature is actually doing the finding for its continued, moment-by-moment, survival via unity.

> "I am sharing space with others who are trying to enjoy nature. I look around, and it doesn't even seem that way. Their actions aren't ACTUALLY connecting them with nature. They are travelers with their gadgets and new gear, and they even hide behind their cameras (phones) when they are appreciating what they see." ~ **RWE participant interaction**

In addition to thirst, we have 53 other senses, each with a similar ability to accomplish this homeostatic balancing act, yet we consciously learn to only recognize and work with five of them. This loss of 85% of our global equilibrium ability is the core of Earth Misery. When I explained this to Senator Albert Gore in 1989, he, like the workshop Directors, was flabbergasted, and the Jack in him still neglects to use RWE to help bail us out of our Earth Misery troubles. It is not part of the *Green Revolution*. I say, "*Hit the road, Jack!*" He did, however, mention my work in his book *Earth in Balance.*

> "The expert said that if there isn't a word for a feeling, we can't always describe or acknowledge it. I immediately thought of our work here and the 54 senses, we are only taught 5. No wonder we (as a general population) can't relate to and describe what those sensations are. I believe we feel and notice all the senses, but the climate of the modern-day world just doesn't focus on being that intricate with being in touch with them. Make sense? Maybe if we spent more time '*being*' in our senses, we could spend more time in RWE and thus, homeostatic balance." ~ **RWE participant interaction**

> *Science is the attempt to make the chaotic diversity of our sense-experience correspond to a logically uniform system of thought.*
> *~ Albert Einstein*

As noted, the great trustable truth that shocked the Directors consists of a seamless RWE blend of 54 natural senses and 24 evidence-based facts. Ignoring or falsifying any of them misinforms Jack, and this lets our speeding car continue to produce Earth Misery. Concerning actualizing a reliable global solution for reducing Earth Misery, each of us is locked in the house that Jack built until we apply our great RWE truth.

> "This particular exercise made me aware of good childhood memories, and I connected these memories to the present good feelings. I often have flashes of contentment when I think of a good memory. An example for me is, at times, I get a felt-sense of a shift in the atmosphere, or smell or belonging and community, and where I can get in touch with time, I felt good inside as a child (paternity and raising young). Before I got involved with RWE, I do remember growing up and going into nature very often when I was having a rough time in my life. I always felt better having done so. I think now I understand that each time I was attracted to nature, I was in need of healing a part of myself. ~ **RWE participant interaction**

The Roots of RWE

🌲 All below:

Workshop Member: *What evidence do you have that shows RWE can help make a significant contribution to reducing Earth Misery?*

By trial and error, and without defining all of them, I, and my expedition learning process, in natural areas, learned how to apply 24 RWE evidence-based facts, year after year, for 16 years following 1969. Each year, each new expedition group first-hand experienced and validated new facts using our 54 senses.

> "In this grassland, I witnessed and reminded myself of the great cycle, how everything was feeling, and living off and WITH one another. I thought about my injured knee and about my upcoming training to be a Nature Therapist. I was worried about my ability to participate with my current disability, but then I remembered the WHOLE reason I want to become a certified Nature Therapy Guide is to get nature to those who can't easily access it. I then felt like my whole knee injury thing is a lesson. Maybe no mountains or climbing is in store for me for a bit, but learning how to sit still again and absorb what nature has to offer is just what I need to REALLY soak in the wisdom. Everything is in perfect balance as long as you have the right lens to look at it."
> **~ RWE participant interaction**

RWE mainly results from the all-year, consensus-based outdoor living exploration journey that I founded in 1959. It's a journey via a specially outfitted yellow school bus that immersed its intimate school community in organic critical thinking, interpersonal experiences, and natural wonders. RWE includes UNE, GTT and the Golden Ratio sequence because it is them in action, moment-by-moment.

Participants thrived from all-season camping out in eighty-three different natural habitats, Newfoundland to California, as well as by expediting their commitments to open, honest relationships with the environment, each other and indigenous people(s), researchers, ecologists, the Amish, farmers, anthropologists, folk musicians, naturalists, shamans, contra-dancers, organic farmers, administrators, historians, counselors, teachers, and many others. The climate of these rich 54-sense experiences connected our inner nature to the whole of nature and transformed our Earth Misery into a unifying RWE love.

As a result of our romance with RWE educating ourselves this way, in the expedition school community:

- Chemical dependencies, including alcohol and tobacco, disappeared as did destructive interpersonal and social relationships.
- Personality and eating disorders subsided.
- Violence, crime, and prejudice were unknown in the group.
- Academics improved because they were applicable, hands-on, and fun.
- Loneliness, hostility, and depression subsided.
- Group interactions allowed for stress release and management; each day was fulfilling and relatively peaceful.
- Senses that had been injured in childhood were recognized as being vulnerable to individuals who, due to similar childhood injuries, were less sensitive to the vulnerability of these senses. Connections with natural areas replaced these vulnerabilities in both parties and increased unity.
- Students using meditation found they no longer needed to use it to feel whole. They knew their truth as, moment by moment, they 54-sense experienced new and different relationships.
- Participants knew each other better than they knew their families or best friends. They risked expressing and acting from their deeper thoughts and feelings; a profound, fiduciary sense of social and environmental responsibility guided their decisions.

- When vacation periods arrived, only a few wanted to go home. Each person enjoyably worked to build this supportive, balanced living and learning utopia. They were home.
- All this occurred simply because every community member met their fiduciary commitment to make sense of their lives by establishing RWE relationships that supported the expedition and the natural world within and around them. We hunted, gathered, and practiced such relationships; we organized and preserved group living processes that awakened our natural wisdom. We explored how to let Nature help us regenerate responsible relationships when they decayed.
- The secret to our expedition's success was to learn to 54-sense blend into and learn directly from the natural world, the life of earth within and about us. Through our RWE natural attraction senses and feelings, it taught our sense of reason how to trust the life of Nature and how to validate and incorporate its reasonableness.

> "What I learned during Trailside in 1970 was the ability to be in sync with our intentions and needs. That included not needing an alarm clock to wake up at 3:00 a.m. to hike through Bryce Canyon in the moonlight. It also included being aware of the animals we encountered and recognizing their verbal sounds as forms of communication. Being within nature with Mike Cohen was a fundamental core of my life, and I became a natural educator and healer. Back then, I was searching for what I would like to do or be and my realization came one night while standing in the waters of St. John's Island. As the water lapped on my legs, I looked out into the sea and made one request: "I want to become wise."
> ~ **RWE Trailside Country School participant, 1970**

> "That afternoon, we had finally come to an acceptance of each other, an appreciation of each other's inherent worth, and a special kind of love and caring for each other and the planet that naturally followed. It was a good, satisfying feeling. Before joining the expedition, I had little understanding of

what an "expeditional" school would be like. This is what I experienced this year:

Expedition meant a group of diverse, motivated people working toward a common goal, in this case, knowledge and perpetuation of the expedition. It meant commitment. We didn't come and go as we pleased; we considered the effects of our actions on the functioning of the group as a unit—we made sure that everyone had firsts at dinner before we took seconds. It meant finding a way of making decisions that didn't leave out anyone's feelings. For us, that way was the consensus. By discussion and compromise, we made sure that every decision was one that every person agreed with.

Expedition meant communication. We were at school 24 hours a day, 7 days a week. The walls erected for protection elsewhere were barriers to smooth relations here. We learned to express our opinions, confront others instead of ignoring them, talk if we were troubled. The result? Not a single person was, or felt, unneeded. Each of us knew our opinions were valued, our well-being essential. We found that others liked us, even at our unpretentious worst (best?). We felt closer, formed relationships stronger than many of us had ever known before." ~ **National Audubon Society Expedition Institute Participant, 1982**

"Mike Cohen is a crackerjack teacher. What counts is that his words help us do what we must do to save ourselves and Gaia." ~ **Pete Seeger**

RWE simply replaces our 1969 to 1985 yellow school bus with our global GTT of Albert Einstein's Unified Field. Scientifically, that is the great trustable, 54-sense natural area truth that we hold in common and coalesces us in every moment. Then we RWE share our natural world experiences via the internet instead of meeting in person.

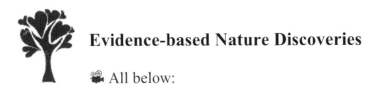

Evidence-based Nature Discoveries

🎥 All below:

Workshop Member: *Being heartfelt, RWE seems to be spiritual, what makes it scientifically valid?*

You can familiarize Jack in the box parts of you with some of the same revolutionary wisdom facts and experiences that helped me and my students benefit from these realities (26). From my RWE white paper at Amazon.com (26), or at www.ecopsych.com/LNE.html.

You can learn by doing while maintaining the integrity of our 54-sense RWE to help reverse Earth Misery.

> "I was witness to a beautiful oak tree that had been visited very frequently by acorn woodpeckers. This tree would, at first glance, look as if it were out of balance, more holes than tree. But upon closer inspection, it is a work of art, flora, and fauna in concert with each other, the tree standing, bearing the weight of animals using it for habitat, food, and storage. The animals knowing the strength, longevity, and source for living and protection from the tree. I find one of the best things about making connections with nature is that RWE comes naturally when you just take the time to stop and notice."
> **~ RWE participant interaction**

As exemplified by the runaway automobile scenario and the advanced technological progress of our expert, but non-organic, application of science in Industrial Society, to help reverse Earth Misery, the science of the RWE helps our 54-senses genuinely connect our story-based life to the GTT part of us that is the non-story life of the natural world, in, around and as us. This helps us engage in the origins of our civilization's original truths before our damaging stories and relationships adulterated it.

These truths were first discovered in the roots of our society by:

Thales of Miletus (circa 600 B.C.) who successfully **omitted the mystical and supernatural** from accounts of nature.

Pythagoras (circa 500 B.C.) who determined correctly that the Universe **contained a logical, inherent mathematical order**.

Copernicus (circa 1500), who combined math and science to validate that the Sun, not the Earth, was the center of the solar system and that Earth turned on its axis. **NOTE:** 100 years later Galileo was placed under house arrest for life for teaching this game-changing, scientific fact.

Albert Einstein (1930) who used science and mathematics to recognize that **the Universe consists of a unified field** that makes and holds together its own space and time, moment-by-moment, including this moment. Remember, right now, you are experiencing these words in "real universe time," but, **if indoors, you are removed from genuine, multiple sensory contacts with the whole of authentic Nature and its organically balanced integrity in a natural area.**

Our challenge is that our *objectivity* causes problems by labeling as *subjective*, our vital and full 54-sense facts of life, and therefore omitting them. They are neither mystical nor supernatural. Rather, they are undeniable, organic, self-evident, biological, 54-sensation truths. They exist. That is the trustful moment that we experience and enjoy as we read these words here as well as in a natural area while it naturally fulfills us there.

"Nancy, such a beautiful story of homeostasis - that the dock leaf healing to the nettle sting was right there in perfect balance to the nettle and your attraction to it! I wonder if we could be so ready to find the homeostasis around us, how would we divert the big issues like hunger, poverty, political unrest that we are seeing and if our leaders could take from this kind of wisdom, how would their leadership transform? Certainly, a caterpillar has much wisdom to be taken from and can teach us about leading a nation!" ~ **RWE participant interaction**

When we experience our 54-senses in natural settings, free of our Earth Misery way of knowing, we feel peaceful and whole with an open heart. This enables us to let the self-correcting ways of Nature help us overcome the effects of our all our Earth Misery symptoms and abuse and strengthen our sanity as we help the natural world overcome, as only it can, the Earth Misery our excesses promote.

"So, long story short, I see the God I was taught, as being a creation of the human mind and a fantasy in order to assist people in feeling comfortable with having a structure of rules to assure they know what is right and wrong. I developed my own "moral compass" as I call it throughout the years and without the rules of religion. The felt-senses I became consciously aware of through this process was sense #40 sense of humility and #43 as I sensed consciousness beyond myself, in Nature and through #44 intuition and subconscious deduction." ~ **RWE participant interaction**

To our loss, our average, our story-driven lives, on average, live 95% of our time indoors. We live in tune with the authentic life of Nature/Earth for less than twelve hours of our average 620,000 hour lifetime. This includes our nature-estranged daytime mind-wandering time that accounts for almost 50 percent of our waking hours. It includes, also, our dream time and meditations when they are nature-disconnected. It additionally includes playing computer games, watching TV, and/or tranquilizing our nature-estrangement discontents with substances that often addict us to them. It includes 18,000 hours of legally required, impressionable childhood, indoor-story based classroom education and homework.

The reason the Directors and their expertise was dumbfounded by not correctly identifying the most reliable truth of their lives is our normal, but extensive, disconnection from it. It was like they were living in a closet (box) and, for the first time, discovering that its walls were not the real world.

During the workshop, the Directors were delighted to discover that the RWE activities helped them reduce some disorders and nature-prejudiced thinking. This occurred to the startling point that I watched one Director cover her right eye and be so excited that she could see a GTT natural attraction with her left eye which had been blind for decades.

> "Your freedom dance to nature's music in the area that attracted you is palpable through your words. I found my heart quickening as you described your movements that swirly feeling of rotation, spinning like a top. I am happy from it, lighter, too. Sharing love right back. Similarly, Mother/Earth is a continuous RWE dance that connects us all, inviting us all to dance to her tune. Your words are exactly it! We are dance partners. And that is the challenge to stay in the dance. I have forgotten, remembered, forgotten, remembered, and forgotten again and again also. I will dance today."
> ~ **RWE participant interaction**

Similarly, we suffer Earth Misery because most of us live in our society's nature-disconnected delusions. We don't realize it until that truth confronts us like being thrown into a naturally balanced and pure organic pond of RWE reality. Then we must learn how to swim in balance with the natural pond *by learning to do it from the pond itself,* not a book, including this book. A book's story can describe how to swim, but it does not have the know-how. Put this book in a pond, and it sinks.

RWE helps us learn what we need to know directly from the genuine pond through our 54 senses. The *Revolutionary Wisdom* book and course float and grow because we read it while we are in the pond treading water. By getting our feet wet after each paragraph, we learn to swim as we get in over our heads. This lets us master letting RWE habitually bring back into our consciousness the pond's eco-intelligent gifts and ways. These are 54-sense wisdoms that we biologically inherit but have been taught to ignore.

Learning how to support the *health of the pond as it supports us* is a vital part of RWE pond-swimming education. This is because the pond is friendly, it loves and uplifts us. It provides us with proper water, food and climate and is vital for the survival of our, and all, love and aliveness. To teach this, RWE provides us with "swimming in the pond" methods and materials while we are in the water.

Most *holistic, alternative, energy, body-mind, whole life, transpersonal, shaman, spiritual, ecopsychology* therapies and practices do not include RWE teaching us how to swim in the pond and learn from 54-sense contact with its integrity. These practices too often are more like feel-good catharsis than long-term education and therapy. For example, the Director's blind eye returned to being blind upon completion of the RWE activity. **Who knows its prognosis if she had continued with RWE?** In contrast, folks who habitually add RWE to their daily life further strengthen their resilience, livelihood, well-being, and value.

> "Homeostasis is something that I would like to achieve sometime in my lifetime. I wonder if it is at all really possible with so many outside influences? By outside, I do not mean nature. Nature is perhaps the only entity that brings me to any form of homeostasis. So why is it then the Earth is so out of balance? From my experiences and interactions with fellow RWE participants, I have discovered that people chose their paths to homeostasis. In today's society, people lean into materialism, a fast-paced lifestyle, and spend very little time communicating in person. Only when they can surround themselves in nature without the pressure of deadlines, unrealistic expectations, and living beyond their means can they truly find a prime level of homeostasis."
> **~ RWE participant interaction**

The past centuries of discussion and lip service about *living in peaceful well-being* have brought us to today's wide range of Earth Misery craziness and crazy-making. We are given no help and don't know what to do, even though we know many RWE stories about what needs to be done. As we get rewarded for ignoring them, we disintegrate the life of our planet and ourselves.

"After asking permission to spend time in my favorite sit spot at work, I was able to balance my energy from anxiety and impatience to calm and easiness. This was mostly accomplished just by looking at acorn woodpeckers flying back and forth from oak to oak, hiding acorns."
~ RWE participant interaction

"All children are born geniuses. 9,999 out of every 10,000 are swiftly, inadvertently, degeniused by grown-ups."
~ *Buckminster Fuller*

Climate Therapy Summary: Twenty-Four Facts from 54-Sense Experience

🎥All below

Workshop Member: *Can RWE be learned or taught when not in a workshop like this one?*

Once the Director's knew their greatest truth because they experientially validated it, they questioned me for almost an hour as to how and why I had founded and established my expedition education school. This was basically the story of my life, and I explained highlights of it to them. I include some of them here as RWE facts of my life that are also your life and all of life. This may help you trust and validate them. You can then use the climate of RWE to get in the pond or safely drive the car with it. You can own these essentials and beneficially apply them to your life.

Each fact is as true as the RWE fact that you can see this page if you are looking at it, and you are not sight-challenged. I know because I experienced them just like Jack did in his leaking boat. So have you, in your own way, since we are both human and part of the life of our planet home.

If you are not Jack or one of his relatives, you can learn how to go to a natural area, and RWE validates my truths as well as your own. That would unify us with each other and everything else far beyond these words. In the RWE training books, folks do this together, paragraph by paragraph, online or in-person in conjunction with the local natural areas. (26) www.ecopsych.com/LNE.html

> "I understand how you feel. Connecting fully to RWE can take some time. In my case, it was many years. In the meantime, one still has the remnants of Earth Misery, and that is why we are here! On RWE's most wonderful '*Unified Field Bus*!' To fully remove our Earth Misery and help others remove theirs."
> **~ RWE participant interaction**

PART TWO: History: events that created GTT Facts

 Personal 54-sense experiences that produced the 24 undeniable truths of RWE and demonstrate that the life of UNE is the best teacher, counselor, and healer.

🎥 All below:

Workshop Member: *Can RWE help people who are not recognized as trendy or powerful?*

While our egotistical story world heralds the abstracts of its successful citizens, its prejudice against nature often ignores the nature-supportive experiences of ordinary people while they embrace the natural world. RWE helps people respect their GTT in natural areas because that's how I started and validate RWE. I encourage others to do likewise.

My Origins in RWE

In 1929 I was born in New York City's Sunnyside Gardens in Queens, New York, Louis Mumford's advanced city planning *garden community* that was supported by Eleanor Roosevelt, who noted that we lose our humanity if we separate too much from Nature. My family, there, was one of six families who escaped the Russian pogroms and grew up together in conjunction with the New York City, Madison Settlement House, and its summer camp.

You, no doubt, have experienced some of my first six years of life in Sunnyside if you have ever visited a natural area.

- Can your 54-senses now bring into play a good experience that you have had with nature, backyard or back country,

mountain, forest or field, brook, ocean or shoreline, pet, garden, or aquarium?
- Can your senses reinstate the colors, sounds, aromas, textures, or flavors of those moments?
- Did they include comforting motions or feelings of joy, community, trust, or place?
- Was it heartfelt, stress-reducing, enchanting, fulfilling, or spiritually pleasing?
- Did you feel more rooted, safe, secure, or friendly?
- Did it feel supportive or peaceful or help you feel renewed or purified or that you were/are part of a greater whole or being?

If you have felt just some of this in a natural area, perhaps without knowing it, you have experienced the baseline of your life and that you know that you have far more than 5-senses. However, if asked how many you have, you still might say five because Jack has *MacDonalded* you.

Sunnyside Gardens, now a Historic District, was my early childhood home, twenty minutes from Times Square in Manhattan on the IRT to Bliss Street. You want evidence? It's printed on the wall of every Subway sandwich shop.

I already described how, when I was six, my entrance into public school abused my true nature in that it emotionally amputated my left arm by forcing me to write *righty* with a dip pen. While in Jack's box there, the school principal refused to move the inkwell to the left side of the desk for me, especially since a hole for it was drilled into the right side of the desk. I wondered, *what makes it 'right'?* That alone was discomforting.

A *taboo* technology fountain pen allowed me to naturally use my left arm to write and not smear. That restored my peace of mind and my penmanship. Things improved. I became an award-winning student even though, sadly, other school mishaps estranged me from my mother in her efforts to correct them.

"I tried to stay put, politely standing by unshaded tables where we were shepherded, but I began to feel really grumpy because

I felt on fire. Certainly, it was a stunning view, but I could not enjoy it due to my discomfort. I was repulsed by the temperature, couldn't take it anymore. I felt a desperate need to escape the intense, fiery heat so I made a break for it. Moments later, the rest of the group began to trickle over, joining us in the shade of the large banyan trees 10 meters from the tables - to the chagrin of the event planner. This week I have realized that every time I've noticed a *repulsion* from myself or my students, it has generally been around safety or a natural instinct to protect oneself. BUT then I think, that is an attraction to be aware, alert, informed, and safe through senses #25-27" ~ **RWE participant interaction**

Using the technology of a mechanical pen felt so sensible and good that I became enamored to make it happen with most things that I did after that, including my education and counseling programs that became RWE. That feeling became my *maverick genius*, a strong, felt-sense intention to continually love, dignify and support the life of Nature in, around, and as me.

Today, scientifically doing this via RWE eco-arts can help anybody bring their problems and the life of Nature into a mutually supportive balance while in a natural area. This blending transforms their source into attractive relationships as the biological whole of life strengthens its and our integrity by reconnecting our 54 natural senses with their ancient home in the non-verbal love and peace of Nature's beauty and self-correcting wisdom. When we produce a story that validates this experience, remembering the story brings it back into our immediate life.

"As I am writing this, I am attracted to the idea of not needing the story of feeling insecure or of lacking confidence, as Nature just "is" and has none of those human stories we tell ourselves. Well, this was fun! I love feeling good!"
~ **RWE participant interaction**

This truth of my life led me to dedicate myself, at age 15, to being a camp director so activities there could help youngsters and me deal with the prejudice of our society against the myriad of abuses, great and small, of our inherently balanced and sane natural selves. My parents were happy with this early decision. An additional 15 years of academics and living and working in natural areas encouraged me to know myself as a person who was qualified and motivated to make this happen. I founded my own nature-centered expedition-experience summer camp, the year-round Trailside Country School, that became the National Audubon Society Expedition Institute, each a pioneering root of RWE. Since 1959, I have lived in similar mini-playgrounds that I have created for myself. Today, at age 90, I still call, contra dance weekly. I continue to sleep outdoors year-round and hike a small mountain daily. I am not prescribed any medications and look forward to sustaining RWE in this or some other form of life.

"I also learned from comments here, to register the experience itself, the consciousness of being in that experience as my great trustable truth. And part of knowing the experience is breathing. Ooh, already, this online expedition of ours is yielding many lessons! Thanks for sharing and looking forward to your next post! Take care."
~ RWE participant interaction

By design, each of my expedition groups was a justifiable combination of Kurt Lewin T-group encounter processes, Progressive Education, and Alexander Wolf Group Therapy. The latter recognized that members of a committed group subconsciously registered it as their childhood family, and in it, they often felt the joy or hurt of the latter and acted accordingly. In experiencing this in our nature-connected expedition family, we learned how to reasonably express and guide our relationships by adding nature's 54-sense wisdom and 24 facts to them.

When expedition members found that some of their senses were injured or weak, it made sense to temporarily ride on the senses and feelings of others who were healthy in these same areas. This continually made the expedition group a unified whole and helped individuals restore their own balance through habitual RW bonding connections with attractive natural aspects of individuals in the group that was the same in the natural areas that surrounded us. Each expedition was organized so that its members included a wide range of injured sense challenges that unified and educated the group as it reduced them.

"I love this, getting comfort from our "Other Mother" (Earth) is just what we all need. Over my lifetime, our "Other Mother" has also been a father sister and brother to me, too, an entire family. A really perfect place to belong"
~ **RWE participant interaction**

Today, RWE consists of 24 evidence-based 54-sensory facts that my expeditions validated over more than 26 years in natural areas. Each is shared by Nature and people, and they have never been disproven, yet they are continually omitted from our education, counseling and healing. I refer to them here for your edification, not because they will change things for Jack in you. That only occurs when you let RWE help you swim in harmony with your local pond. Then you become a licensed 24-fact car driver. You 54-sense know how and why to apply the RWE organic brake that therapeutically stops our high-tech runaway automobile from creating Earth Misery. Instead, your car composts and recycles that misery into fiduciary relationships that increase person/planet love and well-being.

"It is my first time in this natural area, and, although I came far to have this experience, the experience is not what I expected it to be. The attraction is so strong that I was not able to ask for consent, I had/have an overwhelming feeling of being enveloped -- cocooned by the winds, the grasses, and the endless skies. Horses. It is not just me feeling this… the other people who arrived with me are 'giddy' like we are intoxicated with the place and our strong attraction to it."
~ **RWE participant interaction**

RWE Facts

🎥 All below:

Workshop Member: *Which of your 24 core RWE facts have we learned about so far?*

- ✓ Because a sense or feeling is a truth that registers directly on our nervous system, it does not have to be proven. This phenomenon is a moment-by-moment, empirical, self-evident fact that instantly connects that truth in us with its historical origins in a natural area.
- ✓ My abuse and learning experiences that helped me invent RWE included sensations and feelings of colors, temperature, pressure, gravity, balance, community, trust, love, pain, spirit, humor, place, motion, and self, and none of these are our traditional "5 senses." The "5" also omit our senses of reason, consciousness and language/story articulation that are active here right now as you read so they must be true. Irrefutably, I and others have experienced or observed at least 54 natural sense groups whose energies register our relationships in our sense of consciousness. Folks who do not learn this excessively suffer the limited thinking of Earth Misery.
- ✓ RWE is us, scientifically, 54-sense experiencing the greatest truth of our life by eliminating fiction or falsehoods.
- ✓ For the past century, the intelligence of our educated society has scientifically validated and accepted that all things only exist or happen in the Now. It is the instant the life our Big Bang Universe makes its own space and time, moment-by-moment.
- ✓ The truth of the authentic whole of life is that everything happens at once. We seldom learn that getting in the now and speaking from that experience is therapeutic because that is when we are the purifying life of Nature's wisdom conscious of itself in our words, moment by moment, organizing and correcting itself.

✓ RWE is the truth of us scientifically 54-sense experiencing the now love dance of our life while in the now love dance of a natural area.

✓ We don't live on Planet Earth. By trusting our multisensory self, we register clouds, air, wind, sunshine, sound, flying life forms, and distance above us. These self-evident facts affirm that we *live in, not on,* the life of Planet Earth, in its web-of-life and biosphere.

✓ The fact that our disorders are the damaging results of Earth Misery is accurate because, as a boat sinks, all things attached to it sink with it. We are all living in and kin of the life of our Planetary boat. Earth's deteriorating life is our deteriorating life and vice-versa.

✓ Neither you nor I nor anyone else has observed that any species or thing in Nature, besides humanity, operates through abstracts like our written or spoken articulation of words, labels, sentences, or stories.

"My senses were all triggered --- a sense of light and radiation, senses of touch-vision-taste-smell-sound, sense of belonging, sense of place, sense of motion, sense of depth, sense of thirst and hunger, sense of community, and so many more! But one sense struck me, and I am wondering what this is about --- a sense of timelessness --- like the past and future were all there, and nothing else mattered. This feeling is one where every atom felt ensconced in every other atom. It is all movement and yet no movement at all. Is this what it means to feel equilibrium? Motionless. Timeless. Peaceful. Contentment. Enlightenment. I felt as one with everything that is and was at that moment, and the moments felt infinite. Surrounded by endless skies, *this* is the dream. And it is Now."
~ RWE participant interaction

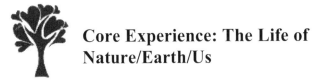

Core Experience: The Life of Nature/Earth/Us

All below:

Workshop Member: *What made you know that Planet Earth was as alive as you or I?*

RWE results from my key GTT with my Planet because in the GTT of that now space/time moment, my personal life's GTT aligned with the GTT of the life of Earth. In time, this identified and then corrected this critical difference between them: I could speak with word-stories, and the Planet could not. The GTT of RWE organized itself as I applied that core Truth to my already described expedition group relationships that sought it in natural areas. Today, RWE enables anybody to do the same, backyard or back country.

August 22, 1965, thirteen years before the Gaia Hypothesis was published:

Deep in the bowels of Grand Canyon National Park, a spectacle of color and towering cliffs marks the place where Bright Angel Creek joins the Colorado River. There, in 1965, a thunderstorm on a broiling August day cracked my twentieth-century prejudices about life and the land.

To keep cool in this desert country, I hiked shirtless. Occasionally, I munched potato chips to maintain my body's salt level. As I did when I earlier passed Phantom Canyon as I crossed the bridge spanning muddy Colorado, my hand again touched my surprisingly icy stomach while the air temperature was 120 degrees. My years of scientific training went to work: "*This is a cooling mechanism. Evaporating sweat molecules carry away excess body heat, leaving this residue of salt on my skin.*" It never occurred to me that the essence of life, not just molecules, maintained my inherent body temperate while the sun-scorched the world about me.

Thunderclouds moved in from the southwest. *"Now you're going to see something amazing,"* I told the twenty expedition members who accompanied me. *"As the thunderstorm rains, the heat evaporates the raindrops. We'll see the rainfall, but we won't get wet down here."* We were a mile below the rim.

I knew this would happen. It had happened almost every year on this outdoor learning trek, which I inaugurated in 1959. The expedition students looked skeptical, but the prospect of a "dry" storm excited them.

The dark clouds rolled in and poured freezing torrents, drenching us while we stood agape. *"Hey, look, everybody, I'm really dry,"* taunted one soaked girl, while smirking group members scurried for cover, gleefully mumbling, *"Oh sure, Mike, it never rains in the Grand Canyon."*

How often those words would assail me that summer and, in the years, to come. Somehow, most students I worked with heard about the incident. Whenever I came close to predicting anything, I'd hear, *"Sure Mike, and it never rains in the Grand Canyon."*

But the skies opened up and rain it did. Quickly the canyon cooled. Like soap suds rinsed from shampooed hair, the red sands and clays of the Grand Canyon sloshed over the thousand-foot inner gorge walls that loomed above us. Everywhere, blood-red water cascaded, and the roaring river turned from tan to murky maroon. The trembling canyon felt like a vein gathering and carrying blood. For a moment, I sensed we were in a gigantic organism's bloodstream. The flowing landscape seemed alive. And just like my evaporating sweat had cooled me, evaporating rain now cooled the canyon, furthering this sense of aliveness.

As I watched Grand Canyon salts run downriver to the sea, I wondered, *"Why does the sea never become too salty, or the land never too hot for life? This is part of the intelligence of life, it is aware of what it's doing."* Then it all came together as the self-balancing homeostasis of life that in 1929 Walter B. Cannon described in *Wisdom of the Body,* that I had read in 1951.

Later, I put words to what I was feeling. It was self-evident, I could not deny it. I experienced Planet Earth as a living organism that has the will and knows how to help itself survive. I deliberately asked my planet how it was different than me. I could find there was nothing I did as an organism that it did not do except; I could create, tell, and listen to stories. I could put things into words that shaped acts.

> "The process of gaining consent to visit this natural area shifted my awareness from being at a place to being with a sentient being. I became more focused on the nuances that emerged, like reading someone's face during a conversation. Everything was more expressive. My defenses dropped as I felt total acceptance. I began downloading my thoughts, and Nature waited patiently for me to run out of words. In the following silence, I remembered why I was here, and I asked, "What part of this area is dead?" I heard, "What do you think?" "Nothing is dead, it is being transformed."
> **~ RWE participant interaction**

I was dumbfounded. I tried to dismiss the living organism idea, but it hung on for dear life. I thought I was the only person in the world who had ever entertained this notion, and I spent time considering whether I should embrace it and risk credibility or support. I'd be seen as a freak. I would be walking an unnecessary giant step into the beyond. Crazier still, I felt I could take this risk because the life of earth would back me up like a loving mother or family. That was nuts. Just thirty minutes earlier planet Earth, to me, was a dead geologic structure floating around the sun.

I moved onto a crack in the ancient cliff face, and it felt like the warm rocks smiled at me. I asked the planet and myself what part of its life was different than mine, and, over time, I became acutely aware that it could not speak or understand stories while I could. Slowly, I made the decision. I'd embrace and live with the idea that

Earth acted like, could be or was a living organism. That thought demonstrates the power of self-evidence when you don't deny it. I immediately felt like part of me had walked into a different world and married it. It still does. This was 1965, fifteen years before the Gaia Hypothesis. I validated my GTT life experiences as a living research laboratory and ambassador of the GTT of Organism Earth.

What I describe above was, after five years on outdoor expeditions, my GTT attracting me to organize my life so I could discover, celebrate, and verbalize the life of Earth's GTT. Through my sense of reason, it empowered my 54-senses to be scientifically whole with nature in word and deed, to beneficially be seamlessly connected to the rest of the natural world, with or without stories.

In retrospect, my extended natural area time with the life of the planet had engaged me as a 54-sense Avatar of Nature. I was the life of Planet Earth manifesting itself as a human being, me, so I could promote its natural balance, well-being, and peace in human words, because, being non-literate, it could not do this. It did this as me because its life, like all forms of life, was supporting itself. It was surviving by transforming me to be its ambassador, and this felt wonderful so I consented.

In retrospect, for the past 84 years, I have daily supported and strengthened the *lefty* part of myself that knows it is the balanced essence of existence, of unadulterated natural attraction being conscious of things it is attracted to. At Project NatureConnect, RWE enables anybody to do the same reasonable thing, moment-by-moment; to deliberately create space for their GTT to connect with, benefit and learn, from the essence of an authentic natural area or thing and thereby help Earth reduce the Earth Misery our false stories have stressfully imposed on it/us. I recognize the planet and myself as living kin. My personal life is living its life and vice versa when my stories and my RWE family support me playing this emissary role.

See <www.ecopsych.com/birthday.html>

"The part of what you posted that attracted me was this: 'I cannot distinguish what is alive and what is dead here – everything is giving life to another thing. Life is transferring from one thing to another. Life is starting to arise, life is thriving.' I also experience this while in a natural area, that the boundaries between objects are blurred. We have divided up the things we see into plants, bugs, soil, animals, air, water, etc. However, if blurred together, without the boundary of our label, then we could just call it all life, maybe? A piece of decaying material is soil, which is alive, which also is a plant, which is also rock and water?"

~ RWE participant interaction

To survive, the wilderness and I share the challenge of becoming too hot, cold, salty, or toxic. The living planet's biology, geology and chemistry are its metabolisms; night-day, night-day, night-day its heartbeat. Warm evaporating inland seas serve as kidneys; air and water are flowing blood and plasma. In congress, all aspects of the life of Earth compose a planet-size intelligence, a wise gigantic self-regulating plant cell whose life approaches the perfection we sometimes call paradise.

Our planetary cell knows how to organize, preserve, and regenerate itself, and how to create and sustain its diverse life without pollution, war insanity, or loneliness. Perhaps Organism Earth is a fertilized egg of the universe. It is the only life of its kind that we know. As such, it deserves protection under the Endangered Species act. **Self-doubt possessed me.** It was sixteen years before I heard of the Gaia hypothesis [3], three years before James Lovelock even conceived it.

My understanding of Gaia grew as I learned that every eighty million years the salt content of the sea doubles, but the sea never becomes more saline; Mars and Venus, the two planets surrounding Earth, become warmer as the sun gets hotter, but Earth's temperature stays within limits necessary for life's existence. Our atmosphere maintains oxygen in amounts neither too great nor too small for all

---

[3] ttps://www.ecopsych.com/en.wikipedia.org/wiki/Gaia_theory_%28science%29

life to survive while not enough for rain not to stop forest fires. Earth's life was supporting its web-of-life and vice-versa, and both grew stronger in the process. That seemed reasonable because, in RWE's whole-life science, *the purpose of life is to support life.* The life of Earth has the same attraction and direction as our personal and collective life, to survive. So does a newborn child and the *Tree of Life.*

> "Thinking that whatever I heard had scurried off, I turned and saw a most magnificent fox, and he was doing exactly the same thing as me, standing, still as a statue and just watching. He, too was no doubt taking in every detail of his surroundings and he had very obviously seen me. I spoke gently to him, knowing that it did not matter what I said, he just needed to hear the comforting tones which said, it's fine, I am not going to hurt you. I did not want to startle him into a panicked run. I was also planning to begin walking away so that he knew that his area was 'safe' when he opened his mouth into a relaxed grin, wagged his tail in a manner akin to a domestic dog and trotted away from me. My presence obviously accepted by him as fine. I knew at that moment that we just had this amazingly intelligent communication, without words, yet both clearly understand the intentions of the other."
> **~ RWE participant interaction**

Scientific investigations continue to validate what I felt-sensed that day in the Grand Canyon. They show that life as we know it will succumb to pollution, chemical and physical forces, and transform into parts of other life forms. For its integrity to survive, it needs the grace and self-correcting, purifying powers that help it balance, restore, and recycle itself.

Recent findings indicate that Planet Earth's biology, physiology, and geology are tightly linked into a single indivisible attraction process that resonates within and about us and can reasonably register in our thinking through the science of RWE. '*Organism Earth*' not only shows signs of life but also registers itself in the life of our natural mind, senses, and feelings as it self-creates its time and space. As already exemplified, its water cycle includes us through the life of our natural senses of thirst and excretion, along with 52 others.

"As I walk through this forested area, I'm searching for what is dead. I see fallen leaves, twigs, large trees uprooted, and the longer I look, the more I see moving, crawling, floating, swaying. There is also stillness – a lot of stillness. But every last part of what is here is connecting to whatever is near it. Either layered on each other, or sitting on another, or crawling on another, or other things growing out of it. I cannot distinguish what is alive and what is dead here – everything loves giving life to another thing. Life is transferring from one thing to another. Life is starting to arise, life is thriving. What I think about when I see this continuum of life is how loving to live is in constant movement in, out, thriving through my life. There are people that have come, gone, thriving, transitioning in, transitioning out of my life, and my heart. Love is alive within and around me, and I experience it through all its continuous movement. I am grateful for this."
~ **RWE participant interaction**

In 1985, a *National Audubon Society International Symposium* was convened at the University of Massachusetts based on my insistence that Earth had to be a living organism. Over 116 presenters concluded Earth displayed all the attributes of a living organism, including consciousness. Nobody was interested in presenting facts that proved beyond a reasonable doubt that Earth was dead. Do you have any such facts? If so, it is a false impression. You'll never be able to prove it because the self-evident life of your/our 54-senses in concert register it as senseless, not real. Keep in mind that whoever taught you or supports that dead earth notion also continues to produce Earth Misery. Remember, too, that you can let RWE help your Earth Misery recover by jumping out of Jack's Box and into natural area RWE.

In 2010, *The People's Conference on Climate Change* defined the rights that our planet should have as a living being. However, contemporary thinking has yet to recognize that RWE offers a 54-sense climate therapy tool that enables us to *implement*, letting Mother Earth help us give her these rights and then act accordingly.

Today, all the living earth information and energy, above, blends together via the RWE methods and materials in my many books and web pages. They help us validate our personal nature-connection experiences as I did in the Grand Canyon. We can sense and feel that we each have two ways of knowing and being 1) our abstract, literate story-telling way, and 2) our ability to grow relationships based on our attractive, 54 felt-sense, facts of life. It is as if Planet Earth is our other body, a foreigner, because it does not speak our language.

> "I could distinguish and identify nature's ability to educate others about RWE. It reminded me about how my tongue thought it talks, it is not done on its own but by the influence of consciousness. It moves along the teeth for any particle and does not go away until the teeth and gum are cleaned. It tests food – sour, sweet, bitter, and salty; thus, it communicates to the brain with demand for water to dilute or to add more of the food ingredients. Because the tongue is one of the mediums to communicate, it is addicted to the story way of doing things (#45. Aesthetic sense, including creativity and appreciation of beauty, music, literature, form, design, and drama). When non-story thinking combines with verbal story tongue, an RWE benefit becomes therapeutic to the entire body."
> **~RWE participant email**

RWE now enables us to be our word. It helps us create moments that let Earth teach our literacy of senses; we inherently know that our socialization teaches us to forget.

RWE helps you validate that a core fact of life is that in a natural area, the self-correcting life of your planet and your life are identical. The only difference between them is that you can speak. You can strengthen your life; via RWE, backyard, or back country, you can learn to sense, think, and speak in balance with and for the whole of life.

RWE activity moments blend the life of our Planet with our otherwise nature-disconnected 54 natural senses. This increases personal, social, and global well-being. However, it does not work for individuals that do not recognize Earth is alive. Jack's box has closeted them to build their relationships with information from a lifeless, mechanical Earth that our *objective* nature-disconnected stories have "imagined" and now think they own. This makes these folks cultural objects, subjects of Industrial Society's irresponsible thinking, mechanics, spirituality, and profiteering along with its other Earth Misery ways of relating and suffering.

> "I am still struggling to find anything that is dead, including a rock. I mean really dead because the planet is the best recycler. Things change physical form, but do they really die? Plants nourish plants, animals nourish animals, humans when buried, nourish the earth. The attraction essence of them is all around, no longer physically here but just back to the earth adding to other life." ~ **RWE participant interaction**

The New York Times: All the news that's fit to print and is 35 years old. How is that new?

The Earth Is Just as Alive as You Are. April 4, 2019: Scientists once ridiculed the idea of a living planet. Not anymore. https://www.nytimes.com/2019/04/20/opinion/sunday/amazon-earth-rain-forest-environment.html

How long will it take the Times to 54-sense validate www.ecopsych.com/journalLNE.html and will the few surviving cockroaches at that time be able to read it, including Jack, the editor?

Historical Examples of Prejudicially Disregarded Recognitions of Earth's Life

1. "The greatest beauty is organic wholeness, the wholeness of life and things, the divine beauty of the universe." Robinson Jeffers, 1935, The Scientist's Visionary.

2. "The spirits of the material universe and plant world are alive, and also more or less conscious. The originating principle of nature is a single material substance. (sic: the Higgs Boson, 2012)." Thales of Miletus, 580 BC, Father of Science.

3. "The Universe is a single living creature that encompasses all living creatures within it." Plato, 420 BC, Father of Philosophical Idealism.

4. "The globe of this earth is not just a machine but also an organized body as it has regenerative power." James Hutton, 1788, Father of Geology.

5. "The whole universe in its different spans and wave-lengths, exclusions and developments, is everywhere alive and conscious. There is one fundamental stuff." William James, 1887, Father of American Psychology.

6. "Evolution is a tightly coupled dance, with life and the material environment as partners. From the dance emerges the entity Gaia. Dr. Cohen is so right to make the responsibility for living on good terms with Gaia, a personal one. It's always from an individual's activities that good and bad things come." James Lovelock, 1985, Father of the Living Earth Gaia Theory.

7. "Earth and you are the same life. Every year 98 percent of the atoms in your body are attracted to become the environment. New atoms from the environment become you. Complete replacement takes place in 4-7 years, about 8 times over a lifespan. Also, you consist of ten times more "other species" cells than human cells; 25% of your genetics are plant genes; the salinity of your blood and seawater is identical, and Earth

intelligently edits its excessive heat from the sun like we intelligently seek shade." Smithsonian Institute.

8. "Moore's Law notes that genetic complexity doubles every 376 million years—working backward, it means that life first came about almost 10 billion years ago. That predates the creation of Earth itself." Richard Gordon, Alexi Sharov, Geneticists.

9. "It is self-evident. Moment-by-moment, as the life of our universe, grows its space and time, the essence of everything in it is connected and at-one identical with it. Any moment that a living thing exists, including ourselves, the Universe and Earth must also be alive." Michael J. Cohen, 1982, Father of RWE.

10. Jesus said, "The Kingdom of God is inside/within you, and all about you, and as you, not in buildings/mansions of wood and stone or fabricated stories. When I am gone, hug a tree, and I am there, lift the/a stone and me being you will find us." PNC Gospel of Forty Days (*(updated from the Gospel of Thomas)* See Appendix C.

> "What a natural joy to read your nature connection!!! You identify and relate to your 54 senses like they are first nature to you. Like you always have known them, and they reverberate inside of you to be released in these activities to share with the universe. Nature is a great teacher very much at home in you as you demonstrate and live in the NOW! You are growing and living in RWE in wonderful ways that keep encouraging all you work and grow with, including me, as I enjoy your natural style and attention to energizing RWE in everything your touch." **~RWE participant interaction**

Additional 24 RWE core facts found in my narrative to this point are:

✓ Since its life was born, the Universe/Nature has remained alive.

- ✓ The life of Nature and Earth is attracted to continue to live, *to survive* into the next moment.
- ✓ In the life-web of Planet Earth, except humanity, nothing uses or understands our verbalized, literate-story way of knowing.
- ✓ Identifying our 54 senses by name in our nature connections makes a critical and unique scientific contribution that is self-evident, and that increases well-being.

"After asking and gaining permission from a natural area I was attracted to when asking *what spirit, creation, self or God is NOT our organic love-of-love that is found everywhere,* my mind wandered to a client I am currently working with that is in recovery from him being raised in an authoritarian religious cult with his family of origin. In his late 30's now, he is looking back and trying to find his way with his own belief system. In RWE, I validate the God I was taught as being a creation of the human mind and a fantasy to assist people in feeling comfortable with having a structure of rules to assure they know what is right and wrong. I developed my own *pass* as I call it throughout the years and without the rules of religion."
~ RWE participant interaction

The RWE Web-of-Life Model

🎥 All below:

Workshop Member: *How do you use RWE to help "Jack" think like Nature works?*

To help reverse Earth Misery here and now I say, "Please try to be reasonable, Jack. To stop Earth Misery, will you at least add to the house you built, my childhood fountain pen remedy for my left-handed abuse, my 54-sense discovery that Earth was a speechless living organism? Maybe that would help here.

Also, Jack, will you add my 26 real-time group expedition years in natural areas plus another 33 online years I spent full-time helping people reduce Earth Misery by scientifically adding the greatest truth of their life to their relationships.

Jack, does this information help you more appreciate the value of creating RWE moments that let the life of Earth teach us what we need to know, or are you helplessly under the influence of disconnection?

Can you at least understand that during my RWE experiences for 59 years, I have loved to the first-hand experience how the life of Nature/Earth works? With advanced degrees and training, I know how I/it functioned while I was in natural areas, and this reinforces what my left arm knew before I was born."

In 1974, an environmental studies model presented by a specialist in Smokey Mountain National Park led me to surmise that the strands that held the web-of-life together were attraction energy.

I discovered this because I went to an isolated area in the Tremont Environmental Education Center and was somehow attracted to ask it what held it, the web, together. In return, it made me be aware of me in the Now and think, *what brought me to this moment here?* I slowly became conscious that *I am attracted to this place, and this question at this moment.* Since the natural area and I were identical, the attraction was the self-evident answer to what brought me there. Thirty-eight years later, with the validation of Einstein's unified field as the Higgs Boson *attraction-net*, the attraction was validated to be my natural sense #35 Sense of self blended with #54 Sense of whole-life unity, of natural attraction as the singular, love of love essence of all our other senses and sensibilities.

Based on Vladimir Vernadsky's 1929 identification of the biosphere, Eugene Odum's *Fundamentals of Ecology* (1951) and John H. Stoer's 1953 ecology classic, *The Web of Life,* experts in many disciplines have accurately portrayed nature and the web of life as I did in the Director's workshop.

I had the Directors find an attraction in the natural area where we met, then make a circle and in it represent some part of nature, a bird, soil, water, a tree, a butterfly that had attracted them. A large ball of string then demonstrated the interconnecting attraction relationships between things in nature. For example, the bird eats insects, so the string was passed from the *bird person* to the *insect person*. That was one of their connections. The insect lives in a flower, so the string was further unrolled across the circle to the *flower person*. Soon a web of string was formed interconnecting all members of the group, including two people who represented humanity.

A **new**, *singular red ribbon connected the two humans in the circle.* The ribbon represented that in the web of life, people alone can connect with each other using the written or spoken abstractions of literacy, of our words, labels, and stories.

Every part of the global life community, from sub-atomic particles to weather systems, is part of and should be included in this lifeweb model. Their *webstring* interconnectedness produces the life of nature's balanced integrity and prevents runaway disorders.

Dramatically, the Directors pulled back, sensed, and enjoyed how the fragile string that they shared peacefully united, supported, and

interconnected them and all of life. Then one strand of the web was cut signifying the loss of a species, habitat, or relationship due to pollution or excessive exploitation. Sadly, the weakening effect on all was noted. Another and another string were cut. Soon the web strings' integrity, support and power disintegrated along with its spirit. Because this reflects the reality of our lives, it triggered feelings of hurt, despair and sadness in some participants. We have long observed and objected to Earth and its people increasingly suffering from "cut string" disintegration, yet we continue to cut the strings because we don't know how to use RWE to stop.

> "The breach that contributed to my attraction to these thoughts and memories was a memory in me, a small part of myself that is still healing from the difficult life I have had, and the part of

myself that is still insecure, and lacking confidence in trusting my natural senses." ~ **RWE participant interaction**

I asked the Directors if they ever went into a natural area and actually saw strings interconnecting things there. They said no, that would be a crazy hallucination. I responded, *"If there are no strings there, what then are the actual strands that hold the natural community together in balance and diversity?"*

It became very, very quiet.

Too quiet. Are you quiet, too?

Pay close attention to this silence. It flags a critical missing component whose absence troubles our thinking, perceptions, and relationships. Webstrings are a vital part of survival, just as real and important as the plants, animals, and minerals that they interconnect, including ourselves. The strings are as true as $2 + 2 = 4$, as facts as genuine as

I told the Directors thirst or motion, water, gravity, or sight.that as part of nature, we are born with the natural ability to sense and know 53 (now 54) webstrings, but we seldom learn to habitually acknowledge or exercise this ability. Without seeing, sensing, or respecting the flow of the strings in nature and our inner nature, we break, injure, and ignore them. Their disappearance produces a sensory void, an uncomfortable Earth Misery emptiness in our psyche and lives that we continuously try to fill.

> "I validated my views on Love as being the energy that supports every webstring. I believe that the Field is made up of energy, which is 100% coherent, which we call Love. Love is all there is, but there may be obstacles that prevent us from the experience of that love. Those obstacles are different expressions of fear. Fear results from believing some nature disconnected story. In our confusion and disconnection, we fail to realize the perfect wisdom and balance of this web, where we are always lovingly guided to

the experience of coherence.
~ RWE participant interaction

No substitute has yet been invented that replaces the real thing. The detrimental side effects of the replacements we invent are garbage that often increases Earth Misery. Authentic Nature does not produce the garbage that we call side effects.

A bird's attraction/love for food (hunger) is a webstring. So is the tree's attraction to grow away from gravity and its root's attraction toward it. The fawn's desire for its mother and vice-versa are webstrings. Every atom and its nucleus consists of, expresses, and relates through webstring attractions as does every kind of material or thing. All of nature, including us, consists of these attractions (14). They are webstrings, basic natural loves we hold in common with the natural environment and each other.

The strings register in us as 54 or more natural motivating senses. As we learn to ignore or subdue them, they end up hurt and frustrated in our subconscious mind. Stored there, we don't feel their pain until some pushed button triggers it into our awareness, and then we may act out on others what abused us to get rid of the pain, or we tranquilize it with addictive technology satisfactions or drugs.

> "The black tadpoles floating on the water gives therapy to my impaired right eyes vision when it does exercise by following many creatures' moves in hundreds in the water makes the eyes muscles relaxed. The pain I felt this morning disappeared. The swinging branches and the leaves' reflection images on the ponds surface and the movement of lettuces calm my worry for rent bills to my place of residence (#29 Sense of play, sport, humor, pleasure and laughter, #48 The capacity to hypnotize other creatures)."
> **~ RWE participant interaction**

We often guide and limit our lives around our fear of being *hurtfully triggered* or hooked.

I noted that this disconnection was very dangerous because it was self-evident that *to be part of a system a thing must be in communication with the system and vice versa*, otherwise they trespass rather than support and balance each other

Similar to a spider web, each webstring is connected to the whole of the web and is attracted and sensitive to it. And, as with the spider and its web, when you touch one string, all the strings become aware of your touch and lend support to the touched string, giving it resilience. The spider also registers an awareness that the web has been touched for its sensitivities, and consciousness is also webstring connections that support the web and vice versa.

Genuine RWE webstring contacts in natural areas enable us to sentiently and consciously reattach the webstrings within us to their nurturing origins, their continuum in the web of life. We feel, enjoy, and trust this thoughtful connection and its wisdom. It is rewarding.

> "The death of a loved one is difficult, we let our senses and emotions take over completely, and we often forget about life. The continuous circle. I watched my daughter and my parents die, two of them slowly. Returning my daughter's body to the ground was one of the most difficult things I have ever had to do, but when I took time to breathe and think, I realized, she is still part of the planet, she has nourished the plants and trees above her, her grave is home to insects and small rodents (she would have loved this thought, she adored animals of all kinds). Her Charlotteness is present in the air, in the Earth, and in my memories. Her ability to share stories physically died but she is still very much alive."
> **~ RWE participant interaction**

Self-evidence in a natural area scientifically validates that the life of Nature/Earth consciously loves to love itself into being its time, space, and us, moment-by-moment. The only thing that is dead is any story that says that death exists. That story part of the life of the Universe argues its point and becomes suicidal. Death would produce garbage. None exists in Nature because death is a human illusion that omits Nature's love to support its life by recycling it into new living attractions.

Webstring connection activities also help people translate webstring attraction feelings into verbal language and share them (through the red ribbon). In this unifying way, our sensory connections with the web feelingly express and validate themselves in conscious thoughts and words that strengthen our human reasoning and relationships. These communications enable us to think in unity, like nature works. We enjoy nature's grace, balance, and restorative wisdom as it continually flows into our mind and relationships. It recycles the contamination of our thinking and feeling into supportive attractions and relationships, like nature works.

> "Your memory of going to nature as a child resonates in me so strongly! Those times were some of the most wholistic experiences I had and still have. They play off each other and strengthen the whole of who we are by filling the hole industrialized living keeps putting us in of despair, doubt, and debt. I think much of my life I was too busy to remember the homeostasis of those times in nature as a child and now that I Grok and encourage others regularly, it is all right here in the now again. I did RWE at work during my 15-minute breaks that helped me be at home in my other body, earth, again and thus at home with myself and others I came in contact with."
> **~ RWE participant interaction**

By adding an RWE, 54, instead of 53, sense version of the webstring model activity, the genuine natural world, backyard, or backcountry, became a remarkable classroom experience, library, and therapist that we treasure (8). It helps us peacefully reduce Earth Misery as we co-create a future in unity with ourselves, each other, and the global life community.

You can't give life without life.
Crystal Faulkner
(Kinfolk to Nobel Prize laureate and
Author, William Faulkner)

RWE and Einstein's Unified Field

🎥 All below:

Workshop Member: *Do you still use and teach the Web-of-Life activity?*

I used and taught the webstring model and only 53 natural senses, not RWE with 54 senses, up to the year 2012 because although it conjectured that natural attraction was the core essence of the Universe, this was also controversial, rather than self-evident. There was no scientific proof. This was because, although he predicted it, Albert Einstein and others could not produce a mathematical equation that established a unifying attraction essence of our Universe. It seemed to be unavailable. Once RWE was scientifically validated, I added RWE to the Web-of-life activity, vice versa.

Einstein was attracted for 30 years, including on his deathbed, to produce his Unifying Field equation. Evidently, he was unaware that his attraction to do this was the Unified Field essence that he sought to identify. It was a 54-sense drive, an attraction/love to find the equation, not just the equation abstract itself.

> "The current position of the sun at midday validates the movement of the earth since in the morning hours it was 45 degrees. I am sharing the colours nature was gifted with because of the light from the sun, the cone, and rods in my eyes. Nature translates the universe's colors, which supports my inner child to love the existing green leave, the red, white, yellow, and purple flowers. My psyche absorbs these lovely colors – yellow for the sun, red for the fruits and the blood in my vessels, white for the space and time as granted to me at the time nature's consent was sought. Colours don't know that the language and names my predecessors baptized them was to validate their conquest (#3. Sense of color, # 30. Sense of physical place, navigation senses including detailed awareness of land and seascapes, of the positions of the sun, moon and

stars and #41 Senses of form and design)"
~ **RWE participant interaction**

In the 1960s, the Physicist Peter Higgs predicted Einstein's unifying field could only be found as a particle, not an equation. The predicted particle was elusive for forty years until it was thought to have only existed in the 180 million trillion degrees Fahrenheit of the Big Bang 13.8 billion years ago or so.

By 2012, efforts by the European Organization for Nuclear Research (CERN) finally succeeded in producing the Big Bang temperature in a particle accelerator in Switzerland. There the particle was identified and called the Higgs Boson, for which Peter Higgs received the Nobel Prize. *In Jack's box*, his initial reaction to the discovery was that it had no practical value. The breakthrough did, however, have momentous value to my 1974 webstring model because it was based on attraction, and it hypothesized that its original natural attraction source would be found.

As soon as the Big Bang temperature began to subside, the Higgs Boson[4] (1) became a net of attraction energy, a Unified Field that pulled, connected, or attached all things together then and after that. It, along with its diverse attraction forces that developed like gravity and electromagnetism, demonstrated Einstein's unified field theory was correct.

From moment one, the unifying field has acted like an alive universal binding mesh that, instant by instant, attracts anything together to clump and grow along with every energy, particle, and relationship that made and is the dance of our universe. It exists. Being moment one, this attraction *glue* is what gives all things that follow in our Universe their mass, unity, and attractiveness including gravity, electromagnetic forces, and us. It is what made matter more attractive than anti-matter to produce what matters today. Each of us is our unique personification of it. Moment by moment, it is our special and collective life-dance as well as our environment. It is the same *macro love* of the Universe to be that its *micro love* binds sub-atomic particles to be. Although micro, the latter makes up for its size in volume as demonstrated by its release energy in an atomic bomb.

Neither I nor anybody else has identified an example of where things are not held together by attraction. This is because what we call repulsion is actually things being more strongly and safely attracted to other attraction relationships in our attraction-driven Universe. For this reason, we run *for* our lives, and in Nature, no waste/garbage is produced. Everything belongs and is what and where it is attracted to be.

> "For this activity, I went to Rattlesnake Creek, a mountain tributary of Mission Creek, which, downstream, has an extensive and costly artificial salmon-jumping project along its route.
>
> Now the salmon can make their way upstream. Once up on the mountain, the fish either mate with each other or with the freshwater rainbow trout that have not yet ever gone to sea. I gain consent from one Steelhead, who was lying nearly motionless to be my partner in this activity. Beautiful is my chosen attractive natural being—big, scarred, time/tested. *'May I remain near you and will you be my partner in a connection experience,'* I think to myself, as I gaze at my Steelhead connection experience through a borrowed scuba mask. Staying with me, and showing me the details of her shiny, if torn, skin, I take her continuing attractiveness as a sign of her consent.
>
> I even re/ask if I have her consent, probably because I am essentially hypnotically attracted. I am thoroughly enjoying what can be best be described as, dare I say it: oddly, initial foreplay in some sort of eco-sexual dance. My senses find nothing repulsive here. Mother Earth is morphing into Mother Lover. Even the remains of the old man-made barriers are attractive because they have within them the impetus for making wise and necessary corrections. This exemplifies how, when a person is properly psychologically predisposed,

a breach in one's welfare, once identified, spawns its own correction.

Trying to stay close but respectful, I skin my shin on the rocky creek bed. Some of my blood flows downstream to the sea along the same course, followed by thousands of fingerlings."

The three aspects of Rattlesnake Creek as my partner are 1) her determination to live out her purpose, 2) her devotion to future generations, and 3) the unassuming peacefulness of her resolution. Now, as RWE suggests, saying these same things about myself seems too self-congratulatory, even narcissistic. It is so much easier to assign my own positive attributes to my Creek-connection experience partner-in-love (30). See <http://www.ecopsych.com/giftearthday1.html>

In using this RWE activity with my clients, when assigning the three positive attributes, they usually do not know that they are, subconsciously, talking about themselves. As I reveal our mutual qualities, circumstances, and fate, a mysteriously generated insight, a trustable truth, comes to me: *'the bad that happens to you is also the good that happens for you.'* Me and my salmon partner have both witnessed the sea. We—in our own ways—are both forever changed by our oceanic experiences. What a release! What a home run! As the Joker in an early Batman movie says, upon first seeing his transformed face: *"Wait 'they get a load of me, now*!"
~ **RWE participant interaction**

In summary, the Big Bang was similar to the sprouting of a natural attraction *energy seed* of the Universe, similar to the *Tree of Life*. Like the integrity and life properties of any seed or the Slime Mold, the purity of its life dance had the natural conscious ability to interconnect, organize, sustain, and diversely evolve-grow-transform itself into being the next moment attractively and fairly. The now of this very moment, including our ability to think, sense, and feel, is the dance of the original seed's attraction to live and, as it cooled, becoming the integrity of its unifying powers for the past 13.8 billion years. This explains why, when we look sensitively, we find   attraction   holding   any   and   all   things   together.

> "Hummingbirds are my Mother's spirit watching over me, guiding me, making me feel secure. The soft singing, the brilliant colors, the intense vibrating sound of the flight, give me a sense of encouragement, stability, peace, connection to my relationship with my Mother, and my role as a Mother. This idea of my guardian hummingbird is not a secret, those closest to me know about it, they don't dispute it. When my friends see me talking and interacting with hummingbirds, it makes perfect sense to them, and for me, it's a reminder that my Mother is still around." ~ **RWE participant interaction**

Attraction is the essence of love. It is the original and continuing space/time life of attraction being conscious of what it is attracted to, as exemplified by a growing crystal. Every moment, along with everything else, it loves itself into being and growing the life of the Universe and Earth including:

- Our attraction to these words as you read them,
- [and/or] Your attraction to going on to the next paragraph,
- [or] Your attraction to something else and therefore not go on,
- Your attraction to breathe, eat, drink, sleep along with 50 other natural sensory attractions including trust, community, and self-help,
- Your attraction to survive as you,
- Your attraction to be and learn in a natural area.

In 2012, the scientific validation of the life of the unified field attraction Higgs Boson core led me to identify a new sense, #54, the sense of whole-life unity, of natural attraction as the singular, *love of love* essence of all things including our 53 other senses and our every relationship.

> "My natural attraction is as a practitioner. My eight years of growing practical, *evidence-based* resources to share with participants in the addiction/mental health field kept me

striving to keep the balance between the two. I thought/think of it as keeping the natural world happy so I can introduce story-based RWE without my clients noticing. Sometimes other practitioners noticed and asked questions, but the questions were always on the positive side of *how do you do that?* or *I like what I see happening with your caseload.* That opened the door to ask questions to help them find their own attractions in nature, share RWE, and encourage others to play with RWE. Balance!" ~ **RWE participant interaction**

RWE Fact: For every new natural attraction diversity, there is an equal, central-binding, natural attraction. This balance of attraction is natural homeostasis. The goal of RWE is to help actualize that balance globally as one-by-one folks increase their expertise in participating in the RWE to produce person/planet integrity. On the first Earth Day, 1970, think globally and **act globally** was not possible because sensory contact with the Unified Field was unknown. So, it became think globally and act locally, but the stories of the locals often clashed. They still do.

Today, our artificiality dangerously separates us from nature's homeostasis equilibrium, its unifying attraction to, moment-by-moment, support both its ancient integrity and its new attractions.

Additional 24 RWE core facts found in my narrative to this point are:

- ✓ Since the beginning, Natural attraction has been free will conscious of what it is attracted to, and everything is held together by that attraction.
- ✓ Spirit, creation, self, or God are our organic love-of-love (sense #54) that is found everywhere in the Now of a natural area and us simultaneously.
- ✓ The essence of all things is the singular now attraction energy of Einstein's unified field.
- ✓ Anything and everything is attached to all that has gone before it and all that follows it. All are always present in the Now.

"Thank you, Don, for these words filled with grace. Tiny slivers of light highlight the space each tree affords to its neighbors. Is that simply caused by years of branch top friction? Maybe it is the result of the sylvan competition for sunlight. There is no evidence of violence causing these barely noticeable breaches in the canopy. Like a group of dancers all too shy to touch one another, the limbs sway in unison. They reveal an uncanny ability to give each other space. It actually seems polite, if not proper. Each tree simply conforms to the needs of those around it. The give and take seems mutual. The space between is remarkably uniform. That give and take, the space, limbs swaying in unison, brings me from the space created to the objects forming, juiciness in their limbs from sap, weighted by their needles. I have experienced this dance in my human body around drum circle others not touching, yet connected through shared space of sound and motion. which brings me back to the creaking sounds of the branches as they are moved by wind.*" ~ **RWE participant interaction**

With the addition of the long-sought 2012 Higgs Boson attraction field, this information should have further validated RWE for the Directors at their workshop, but it was not discovered until 12 years later. However, the outcomes of its absence everywhere else show that Jack has stayed in the Box.

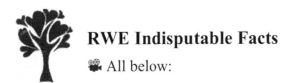 **RWE Indisputable Facts**

🎥 All below:

Workshop Member: *Since science does not prove anything, how can you say RWE is indisputable?*

The truth of our 54 natural senses being natural attractions in action strengthens Einstein's 1920, objective science Big Bang Universe fact, that it makes its own space and time, moment-by-moment. This makes it self-evident that as part of the Universe, we can only experience and know the truths of our 54 senses in an immediate time/space moment. The moment is the only time they, and anything else, exist, including the Big Bang Universe. Hard science also validates this fact, so whatever is GTT in the moment is undeniable, especially without its name or label.

> "I went to a natural area I was attracted to and asked permission to 54 senses unify with it. I asked what my greatest truth is at this time, and had an experience of nature embracing me in the present, and also feeling as if I were in the '*past*' at the same time, back to the teenager that would flee to nature when things got really tough. I was a teen, and I was the me now, simultaneously. I felt safety and well-being. I realized we are timeless as is nature. Nature stands for us day and night, over eons. Nature is there for us consistently, it never abandons us. My sense of belonging was attracted to this, as were my senses of safety, peace, nurturing, attachment, and my own truth." ~ **RWE participant interaction**

Additional 24 RWE core facts:

- ✓ The essence of all things is the singular now attraction energy of Einstein's unified field that holds things together.

- ✓ We often avoid re-living the Earth Misery pain from what has abused us by the relief and satisfactions gained by abusing others in the same way we were abused, or by destructive co-dependent relationships and/or addictively tranquilizing that pain while furthering Earth Misery.

- ✓ There are no repulsions, negatives, or prejudices in Nature; it singularly consists of its stronger or weaker attraction-love dance.

- ✓ The fittest things are the most attractive webstring cooperators with other things.

- ✓ RWE is us evidence-based experiencing our life in the now.

"What was really cool was I gave my sister simple instructions of asking permission of a natural area and then asking what her greatest truth is. She had a similar experience to mine, of the timelessness of her past and present as one in the now. It was really cool! Our child natures were attracted to this experience, and we were jumping up and down like kids and not women in our 6th decade of life! Wheee!"
~ **RWE participant interaction**

RWE Empowering our Story World

All below:

Workshop Member: *Why is our society so prejudiced against Nature?*

I explained to the Director's workshop that when our expedition school community was in a natural area, isolated from our society's warped stories, Nature's truth could be seen easily. I recounted that for a few days, we camped in the winter in the Adirondack Mountains of New York so we could climb them and have fun sliding across frozen lakes. It was 18 degrees Fahrenheit, and we had no water to drink if we did not keep our canteen under our shirt, in our sleeping bag or near the fire because it would freeze. The rangers there would only let us wear wool or insulated clothing.

Keeping warm was on our mind, and our discussions often drifted to our plans to be in the tropics in a few weeks. It became obvious that our Earth Misery problems result from us being attracted to excessively be warm, indoors, in closeting buildings, and that's why and where we live over 95% of our life, on average.

Our extremely nature-separated life is a successful imitation of us originally living in the supportive environment of tropical areas where the earliest signs of human life and art have been found. There, our life and original culture came into being around 100,000 years ago.

As its nomads followed the game or drifted into new climates and conditions, they developed technological survival stories and tools that helped them conquer or tame nature so that the new landscape imitated their/our tropical origins. They applauded their stories, storytellers, and the Gods they invented to bless them while they prejudicially addressed Nature as a foe to conquer for its resources, not with respect for it as the fountainhead of authority in how it loved to produce its balanced perfections including us.

"My culturally framed senses of language habitually become addicted. I have stayed with this story almost for the entire experience of my life. The natural system thinking process of RWE plugged into my psyche to reconnect my disconnected and runaway thinking for therapeutic benefits. My dependence on stories overwhelms the natural thinking each time the industrial economic regimes deny me a chance to reconnect and make my life better while reducing earth misery (#46. Psychic capacity)" ~ **RWE participant interaction**

Today, our excessive artificiality dangerously separates us from nature's homeostasis equilibrium, its unifying attraction to, moment-by-moment, support both its ancient integrity and its new attractions.

To maintain human life, we invented *techniques* that artificially designed and maintained tropic-like conditions for us no matter where we located. For example, the art and science of fire-building provided heat when it was cold; agriculture provided food when its availability waned; strong, stable indoor shelters replaced adverse weather conditions; stored medications replaced unavailable seasonal remedies in the environment.

Humanity became *physically and psychologically dependent* on its wits, stories, and artifacts. The latter became far more important than the vital pulse of nature that, for eons, intelligently sustained the global web-of-life plant, animal and mineral community in balance and purity.

Our socialization increasingly rewarded our psyche with the benefits and monetary profits from artificial survival. This addicted us to human superiority stories and artificiality and to our nature-disconnected leaders, technology inventors, and institutions.

Today, our indoctrination continues to addict us to our creative conquest and replacement of nature's balanced and purifying wisdom of the ages. Our thinking is prejudicially trained to applaud its '*indoor stories and creations*' as more intelligent than, and far superior to nature's self-correcting beauty, balance, and purity.

> "I feel like learning/listening to our body wisdom and learning to connect with what feels good is critical work towards healing. Yes, it does feel as if our society teaches us that the current disconnected society is just the way it is, and almost like you are the crazy one if you think that there is another way to be." ~ **RWE participant interaction**

As greater industrialization has produced greater monetary profits for exploiting Nature, our natural thoughts, senses, and feelings have addicted to *prejudicially seeking financial gain* from nature. Nature became, and remains, an addictive monetary profit resource reward rather than being the essence of life in balance. This addiction is runaway. It has very little to do with obtaining satisfactions from our survival in equilibrium with nature's self-governing, organic perfection. Instead, we gain emotional and economic fulfillment from social prestige, power, economics, fashion, and excessive standards of living that powerfully overwhelm and pollute nature in and around us.

Our warped prejudice against nature removes even our most reasonable thoughts, feelings, and relationships from the healing and purifying ways of nature's intelligent, self-balancing essence (31). See <http://www.ecopsych.com/2004ecoheal.html>

This warp prevents most of us from enjoying a long proven <u>remedy</u> for the *unchangeable* personal, social, and environmental disorders that we suffer.

"I am in awe of the Scientist perspective, and I aspire to understand. While my mind somewhat melts with the physics/science portions, I am intrigued enough to keep returning to those threads, learning through other discussions. Chris's early dialogs/queries about the Higgs/Boson originator particle/basis of attraction theory really helped me to frame out what I didn't understand enough to begin asking questions about!" ~ **RWE participant interaction**

Additional 24 RWE core facts identified are:

- ✓ Things must be valued or measured by their effects.
- ✓ There are no repulsions, negatives, or prejudices in Nature; it singularly consists of its stronger or weaker attraction-love dance.
- ✓ A Now attraction that we find in a natural area is that same attraction in us loving the joy of us consciously reuniting with our self and our unified family origins in the area.
- ✓ The art of creating scientifically accurate, 54-sense stories that are supported by other people's GTT/RWE stories, is needed to catalyze organic change or healing.

Natural Attraction

RWE lets attractions in nature, backyard, or back country, help us bring the homeostasis of Nature's revolutionary wisdom into our lives. A weed growing through the pavement can do it. A park or a potted plant can do it. Our challenge is that being in Jack's Box has taught us to be prejudiced against Nature and, therefore, not get out there and do it.

For example, I participated in a hurried, almost stressful training program for people whose differences kept them arguing and in conflict amongst themselves. They had little interest or time to hear an explanation from me of the unifying and healing benefits of the GreenWave-54 reconnecting with nature process, so they omitted it from their agenda. Amid this hubbub, a young bird flew into the meeting room through the door. It could not find its way out.

Without a word, the behind-schedule, quibbling meeting screeched to a halt. Deep natural attraction feelings for life and hope-filled each person for the moment. For ten minutes that frightened, desperate little bird triggered those seventy people to organize and unify with each other to safely help it find its way back home through the entry door harmoniously, supportively.

Obviously, neither a teacher, preacher, or politician was present to educate these leaders about the value of the bird's life and supporting it. Although it said not a word, the bird, nature itself, was that educator. RW non-verbal sensory attraction factors within the integrity of its life touched these same factors in the lives of the leaders. That contact sparked into their consciousness their inherent natural feelings of love in the form of nurturing, empathy, community, friendship, power, humility, reasoning, place, time, and many more of our inherent 54 natural senses. That reconnecting moment with nature engaged and nourished a battery of their natural sensitivities and sensibilities. These inborn intelligences led a contentious group to support rather than deny the life of a bird, and to bring a new joy to their personal and collective lives for a short period. Yet when they accomplished this feat, Jack's box had them *cheer their role, not the role of the bird.* They felt like heroes for the moment for setting it free and congratulated their humanity for its wisdom and compassion in this effort. In their story of the incident, the role and impact of the bird went unnoticed. They returned to the hubbub of the meeting as if nothing special had happened. They completely overlooked that the bird had united them while it was there, something they continued not to do without its presence. Nor did the bird produce the Earth Misery they were trying to deal with.

I wanted to say something about the effect of the bird, but I didn't. People would have scoffed, as they still do now; maybe told me I only knew what Jack knew. They would have said that what happened was not important or useful, for it was uncommon to have a wild bird interrupt their lives. Their prejudicial story applauded their *human spirit*, not its RW origin and development in nature, even though several Native American groups were part of the training program.

"I was attracted to a further understanding that we have trouble changing controlling situations because; we were not involved in building them, and *We are unaware of the experiences, fears, reasoning, and process used by demanding people to construct or modify the stories; that direct us.* We were not asked to place their stories into our heads, but certain people and societal influences forced them upon us. It is helpful here to have this stated and more light shed. Releasing from old patterns, I feel, is truly one of the most challenging things to break free from, especially as you mention those things from childhood that were truly out of our control. I see how this all takes focus and practice, and trust my natural way of being to guide me."

~ RWE participant interaction

Additional RWE core fact:

✓ The art of creating scientifically accurate, 54-sense stories that are supported by other people's GTT/RWE stories, is needed to catalyze organic change or healing.

Sensory Magic

🎥 All below:

Workshop Member: *Why are the wonderful magic and miracles that we believe destructive with respect to RWE?*

When I was a child, a magician visited our elementary school and explained that he was going to perform a miracle: "*Miraculously, I am going to make something from nothing,*" he said. He first rolled up his sleeves, then opened wide both his hands and twisted them so we could see them, back and front. He asked us if we recognized that they were bare and empty. We agreed. They were. No doubt about it. The others and I, including our teacher, saw this with our own eyes.

Then came the miracle. Out of nothing, there came something. The magician made a loose fist with one hand and with the other hand, he pulled from his fist many scarves of different colors. While he was doing this, he repeated, "*You see, I have the power to make the impossible happen.*"

We all believed in his story. Why not? We experienced it; we saw it. The magician said he could perform magic, why should we not believe him? He certainly didn't lie; he did what he said he would and could do. This built and established our trust in him.

Sight, sound, and understanding stories are just a few of the 54 natural senses that our body and spirit inherit to register the world around and in us. If the magician's label or story had been honest or had his integrity invited us to come closer or touch and feel his hands, we would have known what we needed to know about his miracle. Our senses would have been able to register that he was deceiving us. He would not have corrupted our thinking into trusting him. This is similar to our misguided stories of God, Nature, Love, and Honesty excessively covering up our inborn GTT from us.

> "I love nature, yet I have a hard time verbally to explain why. The conflict and tension I usually live through is calmed by nature's teaching/guidance. I connect with a desert rat that adapts to shades and sour juices from cactus plants. It enjoys therapeutic living because it is immersed in a nature-connected life. I have learned and feel good about myself as a natural being without meeting challenges into my awareness (#25-27 are attractions to seek additional natural attractions to support and strengthen well-being. Attractions to run for your life)"
> **~RWE participant interaction**

Corruption is authority plus monopoly minus transparency.
- Author Unknown

About sixty years later, I became aware of the magician's secret. He had an imitation, hollow plastic thumb placed over his real thumb, and he knew we didn't know this. Inside the hollow plastic thumb, there was space enough to hide the scarves. So, while his fake-thumb was buried in his fist, he pulled his real thumb out from its plastic cover. With his other hand, he took the scarves out of the plastic thumb shell while telling us corrupt stories about his miraculous powers and empty hands.

Why did the Magician mislead us, innocent youngsters? Because he was paid to do it or he liked to do it, it gave him notoriety or power as a professional magician. Somehow it was attractive and rewarding. (2)

Fooling people is how magicians make money and gain prestige. It is entertainment as well as a way the economy works to satisfy our need for entertainment, be we magicians or their audience.

As long as I trusted the magician's label or story, I did not get all the facts that I needed. He did nothing to help me think as a child that he was a fabricator or help me figure out his use of a fake thumb. He did not encourage me to *impolitely* not trust his word or demonstration, to demand that he let me fully experience his hands through my many inherent sensory ways of knowing.

As a consequence of the Magician withholding information and misleading me, I ended up believing in magic.

I don't believe in magic anymore. What I find is that the magician's artificial thumb hides the RWE fact that whole life, self-evident experience, is the best teacher and that scientific research supports my multi-sensory experiences with nature.

RWE establishes until proven otherwise, that the life of our Universe and its Unified Field attraction essence loves to grow its own time and space, moment by moment. This attaches us and the rest of the web-of-life to each other along with all that has gone before us and all that follows.

"I enter the well-designed courtyard, which has many plantings, a water feature, and ask for permission to engage. As I look out at the space, a grassy area besides some sprouting bulbs, under a budding tree attracts me to lay out my mat and foam roller and stretch out in a restorative yoga pose. I smell the spring as I breathe deep, with each breath relaxing a bit more of my body. I am tense. My morning has been tense. My students are tense. My coworkers are tense and I find myself struggling, fighting, to relax into the moment.

Suddenly I sense the energy created in the budding of new leaves, of sprouts attracted out of their bulbs, through the dark earth towards light and heat radiated above. My body relaxes as I consider the great efforts of all the transitioning love of life around me. I feel supported in my transitioning. There are no negative attractions, as we are all coconspirators in our attempts to evolve and thrive. I thank the courtyard for holding space and for sensing me through attractions of interconnectedness. I feel in my being, I am not alone. I am thankful for being guided through physical tension, emotional tension, and on the brink of spiritual tension into unified acceptance of this moment shared.

While I still feel the urgency to meet my responsibilities, I no longer feel that knot in between shoulders that I entered the courtyard with. I sense from the courtyard mutual respect. Being validated from the courtyard's new growth, I provided the courtyard's new growth with validation and protection. I tell myself, '*I am a person who experiences good feelings by sensing into the NOW of space, and then engaging once permission is provided through RWE 54 attractions.*' As I deepen my practice in the NOW of service provision, I validate ways in which the professional can actively engage in RWE supportedself-care." ~ **RWE participant interaction**

Space/Time Travel: Camera-78 and its UNE Film.
Our Intellect: Reason, Literacy and Consciousness

Workshop Member: *How do you validate the fundamental that switched you on to the RWE track?*

🎥 The source of RWE is my Grand Canyon discovery that, except for my ability to speak, Earth and I were identically alive, and our fictional stories about the UNE natural world are what make us suffer Earth Misery rather than enjoy how Nature works. RWE is too often ignored because our high-tech world is dominated by beliefs and acts that eviscerate the natural world. Fortunately, factual stories from trustable authorities counteract fiction.

For example, some folks did not believe the *Yes* results of my 1985 *Is the Earth a Living Organism* symposium until 35 years later when they again read its eons in N.Y. Times article *The Earth Is Just as Alive as You Are,* where it was published as an opinion (32).

Because media makes an impact, I recently produced a documentary film about REW using the imaginary, advanced artificial intelligence of Camera-78 to record the life history of our space/time Universe. It could be considered the **RWE Intellect.**

Because the film is imaginary, I place the 🎥 on each part of it that makes the film RWE valid and 24 facts accurate so its truth will organically help us come to our senses and reduce Earth Misery. This makes the film '*peer-reviewed*' by members of the web-of-life plant, animal, mineral, and energy community since the essence of each of them is included in its space/time moments.

🎥 The facts in this film let its viewers watch RWE from its beginnings because it follows Carl Sagan's advice, "If you wish to make an apple pie from scratch, you must first invent the Universe." I should name Film-78, *"Earth is a Loving Organism."* It is far more than a NY Times opinion as it centers on my International Journal of Physical and Social Science article *The Scientific Core of all*

Known Relationships: Attraction is Conscious of What it is Attracted to. See <www.ecopsych.com/66IJMRA-11702.pdf>

📽️ To help our nature-estranged ego and thinking get a true perspective, I shoot the film on a make-believe living robotic living *'Camera-78'* that records everything at once. That is because its Film-78 registers 54 natural senses (Appendix A) plus 24 RWE facts of life (Appendix B) to produce RWE 78-fact truths. I placed the camera into a historic period 14 billion years ago, 200 million before the beginning of time, right in the place where the birth of our Universe would occur.

Camera-78 consists of today's advance and projected artificial sensors and intelligences that imitate or surpass those of a human being. My sense of reason imagined this Camera to help it visualize the history of time and space, including humanity, in the total life of the Universe. This means that 14 billion years ago, Camera-78 became attached to the pre-life of the Universe and photographed its history to now. It produces 54-sense sounds, scents, tastes, and sights from the past that can help us visualize the time/space reality of all the facts we established and recorded in this book. We know that they are part of authentic natural areas and 54-sense experiences there. This makes GTT more exciting than science-fiction because what the camera films are a natural area fact.

📽️ I know I am the Camera's RWE truth because my experiences and reasoning produced it. It helps validate them as such, not simply some academic theory or nature-disconnected story. In addition, Film-78 places my natural world, self-evident truths into any caring person's consciousness, so it is available to them as a true natural area story along with the opportunity to live it. Film-78 truth becomes part of the GTT of anybody that seeks it via RWE.

> "You have the same thoughts as me! I think about how to name this attraction because I experience unity in this natural area contact. I believe we have some phrases for our sense of reason naming certain feelings. I tried to go beyond this naming border, but I couldn't express what I found there by words.

When I get beyond the line, there appears intensive warming uniting supporting sense-feeling within my solar center. It is like Sun, shining through all shades of green living forestness growing up from the wilderness. The only way I can express it is Art." ~ **RWE participant interaction**

🎥 Film-78 portrays to everybody the actuality of what is otherwise treated as fiction, as exemplified by the Lorax, ET, or Avatar. That is a major 78 fact contribution because it helps reduce Earth Misery by increasing unity. It brings the truth of my unique nine-decade GTT to the GTT of others who want to help reduce their Earth Misery by enacting their GTT in a natural area. The intellectual believability of my film helps make this possible.

🎥 Film-78 documents that natural attraction has consciously, non-verbally, loved us into originally existing as tropical life forms. It captures that as we migrated to non-tropical areas, our loss of Nature's tropical life fulfillments made us physically and emotionally dependent on our stories, right or wrong, for gaining critical life fulfillments, including love, that replaced our lost need-satisfaction that we had, year-round, in the tropics.

🎥 My incredible camera only photographs **one frame per year** as it contains and continues filming life's history from its pre-beginning. When the life of the Universe begins its Big Bang orgasm, each space/time moment of it also became an image on a one-year frame of film-78. The film starts showing things we understand today with the birth of the Big Bang Universe 13.8 billion years ago

🎥 Film-78 registers natural attraction to be the felt-sense essence of what our story way of knowing labels or calls *"love."* Each film frame year records imbeds and stores the scientific events and history of each space/time moment of the life of our Universe and Planet to this instant. Each frame contains the information embedded in it that includes and seamlessly continues from the previous film frame. Each frame is also physically attached to its earlier frame by the film's physical celluloid construction.

🎥 The Film-78 sequence is the same as the sequence of our immediate life today and what we know. For example, each now moment includes the information at the beginning of this paragraph, along with the beginning of this sentence to this now period.

🎥 Today, if we watched the entire film-78 in a movie theater as it is projected at 24 frames/per second, (*meaning 24 years/second*) as are most films, we would watch it, all day and all night, popcorn after popcorn, frame after frame, moment after moment, at 1.3 billion frames per year.

🎥 From the start to finish of its representation of 13.8 billion years at 24 years/second would take 10.5 years to end in the present moment.

🎥 As an overview, Film-78 shows natural attraction has consciously, non-verbally, loved us into existing as tropical life forms whose temperate zone stories made us depend on these stories for satisfying our physical and emotional needs from them. These artificial satisfactions replaced our loss of Nature's tropical fulfillments when we live in non-tropical areas.

🎥 Our ego is our story about who and what we are. It prides itself on being accurate to protect us from harmful distortions of the truth. It usually is astounded when it learns from the movie that the appearance of humanity, accompanied by our unique story-telling ability, does not appear in the film ***until the last 2 hours of the last day*** of its UNE 10.5 years of day and night projection.

🎥 In the film, all the web-of-life that preceded our stories/us self-organized (organically) into being Nature's perfection without using stories. Life's attraction for the additional strength and attractiveness from being diverse loved us into being an attractive part of the life of Earth that used attractive stories to help it map the tropics for its survival advantage. This is contrary to disconnecting, egotistical stories that attach us to believe that we are superior to the life of Earth and that Earth's life wants us to be its king or manager, rather than be organic with all.

🎥 Scientifically, every bit of the film is us at any moment, including now, because, like the sequence of the space/time Universe, all things are attached to what preceded them and to what follows them, and the essence of all is the present space/time moment.

🎥 If we exist, the essence of all exists, including my documentary film-78 as a movie story and as RWE in the reality of right now. Reading these words right now demonstrates this beyond a reasonable doubt. This moment is the state of the Big Bang, including our stories, right or wrong, about this moment.

Until humanity appears in the film, it displays:

🎥 On Film Frame 1.
Nothing is seen at the Big Bang beginning; Camera-78 just photographs part of itself because my Revolutionary Wisdom story was attracted *(loved)* to put the camera there to help explain Revolution Wisdom. That it was attracted to record itself being there is my personal story-78. *In historical sequence, this would be the Fibonacci Golden Ratio #0.*

🎥 On Film Frame 2.
In its beginning, all that film-78 records is the free will life of attraction being conscious of what it is attracted to (loves) in order to organize itself more attractively and *organically* support its survival. *In historical sequence, this would be the Fibonacci Golden Ratio #1.*

🎥 The film shows that the life of attraction becomes consciously attracted to give birth to the extremely hot Big Bang, the life-energy *seed* of our Universe, and its attraction to survive by supporting life. (It loved itself into being the *Tree of Life*). *This would be the Fibonacci Golden Ratio #1 (0 + 1).*

🎥 Immediately, attraction is then attracted to have part of itself become a Unified Field attraction/love "Higgs Field," **It is the root essence and source of all that follows it.** As the Universe grows, the field's energy attracts or attaches and unifies all matter and energy as different forms of energy attractions produced over time (Gravity, Electromagnetic, Strong Force, etc.). *This would be the Fibonacci Golden Ratio #2 (1+ 1)*

🎥 Our Universe's Unified Field loves to live by self-organizing (**organically**) growing its own, singular, time and space attractions moment by moment, frame by frame. Intellectually, *The next number would be the Fibonacci Golden Ratio #3 (2 + 1), and this 1.618 increase and sequence continues to the now moment today as you read this.*

🎥 In year 7 of the 10-year film, the life of Planet Earth first appears. Camera-78 then focuses on Earth's life as it is attracted to becoming more diverse and thereby stronger as time progresses.

🎥 The final day Film frame, 10.5 years after it began, shows that humanity and its 54 senses first appear two hours before the film ends, about 130,000 years ago. Our stories, along with the artifacts our convoluted story-brain invents, show up. For our non-tropical survival, we start listening to and heeding our leader's stories more than we do our 54-sense/loves registering our Unified Field attraction essence in natural areas.

🎥 Our story about ourselves, our Intellect and Ego, replace what Nature otherwise signals in 54 sensory/emotional attraction ways. This disconnects us from the way nature's unified sensory love of life loves to correct, organize, and purify itself in homeostatic balance.

🎥 Like a bulldozer in the Garden of Eden, our stories override and overpower genuine, **wild** nature because nature, being non-literate, can't defend itself from them or plead its case. Our short cathartic release for this atrocity is our attraction to violence or horror stories when therapeutic RWE experiences are simultaneously available. In natural areas, our inaccurate stories are unstoppable foreign abstracts that can be **deep state** weapons of mass destruction of Nature because pre-human Nature only knows and consists of unifying attraction energy, not abstract-story substitutes for it. In the natural world, accurate stories are intellectual embraces from and for the Unified Field.

🎥 Our stories attract our sense of Consciousness, sense #43, to disconnect from and then build and closet parts of ourselves from Nature. These Nature-disconnected parts, in turn, are attracted to build, live in, and love the artificial places, arts, and technologies our nature-disconnected stories invent within our isolated, nature-separated world of Jack's Boathouse. That world is walled-off from its non-story origins that at the same time exist in natural areas, moment-by-moment, while our stories *improve* them, so they become our built-environment exclusive of the life of Earth's organic attraction ways.

🎥 On the film, Earth Misery results from the astonishing arrogance of Jack's closeted ego story to applaud its exclusive closet-story existence as **intelligent** and to regard Nature and RWE as a limitation on its unhealed ego need to be excessive. Even as it suffers the Earth Misery that its excessiveness creates, the disturbed ego believes it is so brilliant that, without help from Nature, it can absorb, replace and manage the wisdom of Nature/Earth's life process established at the beginning of time. In addition, the ego egotistically believes that it was created for this non-organic management purpose by some deity that its story also invents. The stressful, nature-disconnected hole and discomfort of that short circuit in our ego's story produces disturbing feelings that alert us to the personal and collective destructiveness of the hole.

🎥 To the ego, being wrong is a discomforting symptom of its invalidity and disconnected abandonment from the organic way that Nature works. RWE threatens it until it learns to incorporate and own RWE as a powerful love tool for nature-reconnected, 54-sense unity. Then RWE makes our ego/self, reasonably look, and feel good because it unifies with nature's love for it as part of its constructive, now oneness.

🎥 In the film, the continually strengthening artificial closets built by humanity, unnaturally but more safely short-term, support our life in non-tropical areas. This unlimited growth phenomenon excessively separates our story-closeted lives from their filmed, prior, 10.5-years of life and the purity of natural areas. Our closeting experience enters our conscious and discloses our unbalanced exploitation of the natural world.

🎥 Increasingly, in the last three minutes of Film-78, our excessively closeted human life is what becomes 54-sense attractive to modern humans. Nature becomes a resource to be runaway manipulated for indoor rewards that include profits. These gains are stressfully and abusively produced by our advanced tools that enhance our closeting. They are the artificial technologies that we love instead of loving Nature, as of old. We begin to see the adverse side-effects of this unstoppable surge of destructive pretentiousness as its excessiveness creates today's Earth Misery.

🎥 Accurate, non-fiction math/science laws, as well as fictional bible scripture, are written 2.5 minutes before the film ends.

In the last 20 seconds of the film, Columbus affirms that the world is round. Copernicus, using math/science, determines the Sun, not the Earth, is the center of the solar system, and Galileo is jailed for practicing it.

The industrial revolution starts in the last 9 seconds of the 10.5-year movie. Under the flag of progress and economic growth stories, its dominant, 5-sense objective (non-organic) nature-conquering arrogance teaches us to deny and excessively exploit the balanced integrity of Nature's eons in natural areas and ourselves while transcendentalists try to acclaim and protect its beautiful ways.

In its last 3 seconds (1949), the deteriorated state of North America is acknowledged, and legislation is enacted to protect its environment.

🎥 As most people today experience, in its last 2 seconds, (45 years), Film-78 shows increasingly dangerous person-planet Earth Misery from resource overuse commencing in 1974 until now. This observation results from the science of Earth Overshoot Day and other research. It painstakingly establishes the date each year that the life of our Planet runs out of the resources that it/we need to survive in balance for that year.

🎥 Since 1965, RWE, an antidote for the root source of earth misery, helps our ego and intellect heartfelt treat the life of Earth/Us like it is our cherished mother, child, or pet rather than fight an undeclared war against Nature that we are being rewarded to win. The effects of Earth's self-protective climate change to maintain the fair and equal balance of organic life results as our climate crisis. Note what the scientific, stop climate-crisis community is saying. Note that they have yet to identify RWE no less add it to each measure that they propose now and as the last 40 years.

🎥 An eye can see everything around it, but it can't see itself. Similarly, the Film shows that our story way of relating is like the singular, story-telling voice of our living planet. It can accurately 54-sense register, understand and talk about the world but not about itself as part of it because story-telling is a different language than Earth's natural attractions being conscious of what they are attracted to. Stories are foreign to the pre-human web-of-life.

🎥 RWE empowers the web-of-life to help our intellect's story-telling ability become a balancing organic part of the web rather than have us be excessive and suffer our stressful isolation that produces Earth Misery.

> "For myself, it has been a movement from early in my life when I went to a Baptist church for some years, then was indoctrinated into the Christian religion with an old God in the sky who judged others. The Ten Commandments was a staple in my household growing up. After my father died, our family drifted from church, and my mother became more interested in what she called the *'life force'* and the idea we are all connected. I, too, began to think this way and realized I was always connected to Nature in a fundamental way. By this time, I was in recovery from alcoholism. I continued to study and read and experience RWE Nature as my higher power."
> **~RWE participant interaction**

Validation of Film-78

🎥The source of my documentary movie is the self-evident GTT from my scientific, 90-year life-experience that includes advanced academic training and 60 years of 54-sense natural area expedition exploration (4). See <ecopsych.com/mjcohen.html>

🎥 The film's RWE essence is GTT true to and identical with the 1925 scientifically validated and established time/space, moment-by-moment Big Bang universe. (27) This means that:

- ✓ The film's facts are real and available in the present moment. See <www.ecopsych.com/mindread.html>
- ✓ Its GTT includes that all things are held together by attraction, and that attraction is the essence of love, an essence that is conscious of what it is attracted to (what it loves).
- ✓ The GTT of the life of Planet Earth is also the fundamental love to be alive of all things because, moment-by-moment, they exist as the essence of one unified, UNE space/time *Tree of Life.*
- ✓ The film is as real in the 13.8 billion year old, pre-human life

of the universe as it is at this moment in natural areas. This is because at any given moment, as oneness, all things are attached to all things that preceded them and all things that follow them.

✓ The film presents evidence that refutes the false prejudices of our hurting, excessively Nature-disconnected Ego and the destructive outcomes of its erroneous stories. (20).

✓ The film exhibits the GTT Golden Rule: correcting or treating our erroneous Ego stories with RWE transforms Earth Misery into unifying love.

Watching the UNE film helps make our senses, especially those of reason, consciousness, and literacy, aware of the root cause of Earth Misery as well as its readily available RWE antidote. In synopsis, this knowledge includes that

- Humanity and our arts and stories begin to appear in the final two hours of the film (approximately the last 80-150,000 years of the 13.8 billion year film record, a super-microscopic percentage of the total film.)

- Previous to our recent two-hour presence, the film's previous three year (*5-billion year*) life-dance of Planet Earth did not need or use stories to fulfill its attraction/love to live and grow its perfection, its ability to organize, unify, self-correct, diversify, cooperate, balance, purify and reproduce itself without creating garbage or abusiveness while producing its web-of-life optimums.

- Earth's love to live, to survive, remains alive in this moment and is felt-sensed as 54 attractions that exist in natural areas and us. As of old, they physically and emotionally are attracted to unify, strengthen, and support its/our life oneness, a unity that promotes balanced survival.

Death consists of our nature-disconnected stories that appear as part of Humanity's last 3-minute section of the film. They are a *myth*, a lie, a fable that incorrectly tells us that death exists. If true, it would mean that, at times, the life of the natural attraction/love essence of the life of the Universe does not exist. Film-78 shows no evidence of its disappearance. Instead, everything else is a form of love or supportive transformation of some part of global life into another, not its deterioration or elimination. This helps explain why the difference between life and death has never been scientifically defined. They are different names for complementary parts of the same unifying love-of-life dance that includes human life without its excessively nature-disconnected stories and acts. As previously noted, all that is really dead is the suicidal story/statement that says death exists and the story parts of people who heard it.

> "Is it any wonder that we fear death excessively when we sense and feel that our other body, life support system is being destroyed?" ~ **RWE participant interaction**

According to the film, death is actually us transforming into the balance and beauty of the eon's story-less, more-than-human form of life climate, like a caterpillar is attracted to transform into a butterfly.

🎥 A contribution of Camera/Film-78 is that it scientifically confirms the '*unscientific, hippy, spiritual*' 1973 chant, "*This is the wisdom of the ages: the **only** truth is love.*" Film-78 makes natural attraction love a wide-ranged, repeatable, and accepted GTT science. It includes that RWE in a natural area helps us remedy the Earth Misery our excessiveness produces.

🎥 The singular oneness-unity-love depicted in Film-78 is identified in some real way throughout most of humanity. However, once it is labeled, it is usually attached to a wide variety of different conflicting stories. This local and global dis-integration produces 54-sense divisiveness and Earth Misery rather than unity.

🎥 Stories are *artificial foreigners,* loaded guns that can unreasonably capture or abuse our 54-senses. RWE is a story-78 that reasonably frees our senses and unifies all things.

> 🎥 In summary, like having an addiction to cancer, our sensory attachments to non-changing stories disconnect us from the

everchanging life of our non-story, global, life support kin and community in natural areas. There, our addiction weakens many unified relationships, and they deteriorate due to their loss of natural attraction, life and love.

🎥 Only when our stories and acts reconnect things and help unify the global life community, including us, do we recover. We accomplish this by adding the RWE process to our excessively closeted ego, stories, and relations.

🎥 Whenever the information in Film-78 helps us achieve the above, it enables us to become more organically expert drivers of our runaway, high tech car. RWE reduces our Earth Misery suffering that the car's excessive nature-disconnection produces and that includes most things and relations since our thinking and lives are already 45% out of balance and counting.

🎥 Camera-78 is real in that it is, in reality, any of us using RWE to stop our misleading stories from hurtfully making us chase our tail.

For example, I was the Camera when, in the Grand Canyon, my intellect asked the planet how we were different. All of RWE grew from that GTT moment of discovering we were the same except for storytelling. Will the film show me receiving the Nobel Prize? No, because it will never be made.

Right now we are Camera-78. We either keep fighting over who gets what "loot" from being excessive or we insteadapply RWE Climate Therapy. Making a film about the latter as we do it will be the greatest love movie ever; will will love that we star in it.

🎥 Camera-78: The Intellect's Conclusion

Moment-by-moment, the life of the Big Bang Universe/ Nature/Earth (UNE), creates its own time and space. The essence of all UNE things is an identical *oneness* because all things happen simultaneously, including us.

• Whatever happens to UNE happens to us and vice-versa.

- When our untrue stories disconnect our lives from the self-correcting powers of UNE, the atmosphere of our personal, social, and environmental relationships suffers an secret war (39). The remedy for the root cause of this catastrophic disorder is the revolutionary wisdom of Climate Therapy.

- Attraction/love is the only thing that pulls together, attaches, or unites parts of UNE great or small.

- On Planet Earth, the UNE web-of-life is speechless except for humanity.

- Heartfelt scientific methodology only accepts evidence-based facts.

- In Industrial Society, on average, 99% of our thoughts, feelings, and relationships are out of tune with UNE. Our 54-senses are facts of life that uncomfortably register this loss and our estranged isolation.

- Each of us is UNE looking out through our eyes at itself without our ability to relate through abstract stories. These stories confirm that we are different than the more than human world and aggrandize that we are superior to it because it helplessly can't speak for or defend itself.

"I can feel the roots in us, an ancient present now calling, nurturing a healthy trunk, flexible branches, deep-reaching into earth's web of life. By all my relatives. I need to walk barefoot! And I did so: stood up from this chair, took off shoes, walked to the garden, stood, rooted, became a round rock laying on the earth, warmed, stood as a trunk, and reached the sky. I can feel and am related to the exhaustion, your/our exhaustion, the fear, a sense of capitulation when confronted with chaos, and a desolated landscape, the loss of hope, and our past stories poking back in mind. I can feel the need to go back home, a natural womb (#50 joining a more established

organism) and to renew, to restart, but not from the beginning). And yes, life has many cycles, as nature shows us in seasons and contrasts. Thank you for reminding me I can accept the moment, and the changes that come, it is only natural. I can live in the dark for the moment and can thank the candle and its light for I am here, sensing, alive. I take a deep breath, my eyes wet of sublime love for life. It inspires me"
~ RWE participant interaction

Be Natural. Think with Mathematical Accuracy
🎞 All below:

Workshop Member: *How and why does RWE improve the accuracy of Mathematics?*

I have searched, but never found, the answer to this simple question: *Why is Mathematics accurate, undeniable, and universal? Why is it the most sought empirical proof in most cultures?* Dozens of profound answers are offered, none to them is correct if it is not RWE. The closest says mathematics is abstract, and it does not exist or it has no definition.

Here is the RWE GTT actuality: Mathematics is trustable and accurate because, moment by moment, it is an exact literacy story. It correctly symbolizes the story-less, 54-sense **sequence** of the life of the Universe/Nature/Earth/Us since its beginning as 'Unified Field Attraction Love.' However, it is never accurate from one moment to the next because each moment is organically different, things have changed in UNE so, just as a tree loses a leaf to the wind and is now different than a moment before, the period at the end of this sentence is not UNE the same as the period of the preceding sentence.

Math reasonably brings into our awareness the latest film frame moment of attraction being conscious of what it is attracted to. It accomplishes this because it consists of numeral symbols that humanity has correctly assigned to the universal, moment-by-moment *succession of the life of the Big Bang UNE* and its unified field. The numeral symbols accurately register its truth on our 54 senses. They honor its factual global life sequel history because that story helps our life simultaneously survive in UNE and vice-versa.

The order of 0 1 2 3 4 5 6 7 8 9 precisely represents life's sequence to this instant, this moment of truth, of all of that, has come before us and all that follows us. Jack in his Box, produces Earth Misery because he excessively disconnects himself from that truth in Nature, so his stories and acts disturb the sequence. For example, by thinking 6 is unlucky and is only worth 5.5 Jack makes the whole-life truth of Math 0-9 a misleading falsehood until the error is corrected in a future moment. When that occurs, it corrects our entire relationship with the history of the eons and its Golden Ratio. To our harm, however, without RWE, Jack, instead embraces 5.5 as a story he is attached to. He can withhold its UNE and then sell this falsehood to the wanting, Earth Miserable public and he tries to box the world in his irresponsible endeavor

For example, an inaccurate Math story is the number 0 when applied to real life without labels. There is no such thing as zero after the Big Bang because it was/is a *'thing.'* What we call *'no-thing'* or empty in any moment is always filled with GTT Big Bang unified field natural attractions between all things that are conscious of what they are attracted to (28). This sequence of attraction phenomenon make UNE a thing.

Zero is the UNE living sequence attraction/love to become *'1'* in the next moment. It exists. This means 0 is not *'nothing,'* rather it is an UNE attraction/love to live that we felt-sense experience as our love to love (Sense #54). We suffer by our story inaccurately giving zero value to the existence of attraction/love when it is actually the essence of UNE/us. Excessive disconnection from it produces Earth Misery. It produces a fundamental insecurity or stress *'hole'* in our psyche.

The Fibonacci Golden Ratio

My 90 years of life experiences with natural areas made RWE include knowing and being myself (along with everybody else) as living and humanizing the history of the life of one Big Bang UNE moment attracted/loving to build/grow its own next life moment. I came to know my life as a personification of that attraction/love.

Recently someone asked me what I thought about the present answers the puzzling sequence of Euclid's 300 B.C. Fibonacci Golden Ratio that no one can really explain (35).

I looked at it, and within two minutes, I provided an accurate GTT answer that evidently nobody has ever seen or expressed for over 2000 years. Mine is this:

Mathematically speaking, my GTT moment at any time is 0, my UNE attraction to live/survive/be in the next moment as a person (1).

1) I then, in the next moment, become the sum of who I am, 1 (0 + 1).

2) In the next moment I (1) then again become the sum of who I am: 2 (1+1).

3) Then again: 3 (2+1).

4) Then that sum: 5 (2+3).

5) Then: 8 (3+5).

6) Then: 13 (5+8).

This Fibonacci sequence *Golden Ratio* 0, 1, 1, 3, 5, 8, 13, 21 ad infinitum is found as a constant in nature, an UNE truth of you and me that is also found in snail shells, pine cones, flowers, and galaxies. This is UNE GTT in action.

The golden ratio is 1.61803399 etc. to infinity. It never ends because the Universe continues to make its own space and time and the ratio continues to convert it into numbers.

I have yet to find anybody else, including Einstein, that can or has humanized and scientifically explained the Golden Ratio as the GTT of UNE living, loving, experiencing, and expressing itself. This is similarly true of some of my 24 RWE facts. (Appendix B).

-Google indicates that nobody has ever asked my Director's Workshop question, *"What is the greatest trustable truth in your life, and it is not Nature, God, Love or Honesty?"*

-Albert Einstein could not mathematically produce a valid Grand Unified Field Equation because the unified field is not an equation; however, my RWE recognized it (11). It was his unceasing attraction to identify it.

-Wilderness values and therapy omit RWE, so while increasing Mental Health, they also increase Earth Misery.

-Omitting RWE from Particle Physics quantum explorations warp its findings because they are influenced by Earth Misery distortions.

- Omitting RWE from Management, Education Religion, and Philosophy's knowledge about UNE's ability to be diverse, pure, cooperative, and balanced without producing garbage increases Earth Misery.

It's a bit scary to me that in my recent first contact with and discussion about the origins or meaning of the Golden Ratio I could almost immediately see and explain it as above and nobody had come upon that realization due to not consciously 54-sense knowing or invoking their GTT love in a natural area. It was like a Deja vu of my Grand Canyon living planet experience or my humanization of the space/time UNE into organic, 54 felt-sense knowledge of RWE and its application as Climate Therapy. These all resulted from me constantly being the instrument discovering the *lefty* GTT of my life in natural areas in order to subconsciously escape the Russian pogroms and support my survival. (Appendix C)

I was identified as a Maverick Genius (34) for my Grand Canyon interest in exploring how my life was different than how Planet Earth worked. That background gestalt helped me create RWE and discovering the 24 facts in Appendix B. This has produced my self-image as me being a personification of UNE. Its value is stress reduction and anger management. For example, a pesky robocall comes twice a day and says, "*Hello World*." I have transformed that annoyance into being a cheery greeting to me from Society because it recognizes me for whom my attraction to UNE has made me become, so, cheered, I thank the robo for calling.

If you can't locate anybody else, past or present, whose life has put together the likes of RWE, let me know. I'll give you the address to have the Nobel Prize sent to me after I send them the necessary postage. (28)

The film frame of this instant shows that, globally, our unbalanced stories and acts have '*unbalanced*' me, too, as well as dangerously produced Earth Misery. Sadly, our prejudice against Nature taboos its RWE remedy to be added to our every relationship.

> "I sense the spring peepers that I cannot hear, but I know are days away. (#31-time rhythm) I sense out to the migrating hummingbirds, which come later in the spring season. (#37 colonizing) To them, I open heart sense out a message of these sensations, a beacon to them. Keep going! You can do it! We are waiting for you." (#30 navigation.
> **~ RWE participant interaction**

Additional 24 RWE core facts:

✓ The art of creating scientifically accurate, 54-sense stories that are supported by other people's GTT/UFC stories, is needed to catalyze organic change or healing.

✓ Anything and everything is attached to all that has gone before it and all that follows it. The unifying essence of all is always present in the Now.

✓ In the life-web of Planet Earth, except for humanity, nothing uses or understands our verbalized, literate-story way of knowing (Sense #39)

"I pretty much embody these 24 facts, and I am also the embodiment of them, so each is also an issue when I express it in the contemporary world that is always there. This is not a big deal since I build playgrounds that I let folks enter when they/I am ready; however, this is limited and sometimes lonely. Sometimes my greatest sense of loneliness has been experienced within the thralls of crowded moving spaces, like grand central station. As I become more comfortable with myself by being naturally re-energized in nature, I become more comfortable in my own skin again, living into the essence of all things in this singular now attraction of the natural world I am in. It often refreshes me and reconnects me with RWE to make wiser, more natural decisions rather than sucking on my soggy sock." ~ **RWE participant interaction**

SUMMARY

 Experience 60 Minutes of RWE

🎥 All below:

Workshop Member: *Are there shorter get-togethers we can use that familiarize people with RWE?*

In 2017 A.D. I designed a 90 minute guided RWE walk that encapsulated parts of the full-day workshop that was done with the Directors in 2000. This walk includes the Camera Film-78.

The following writeup, from a first-time participant's walk, captures, reviews, and updates what occurred with the Directors seventeen years earlier. I expanded the walk to include the 2012 Higgs Unified Field.

While I was in a protected natural area near Guss Island, learning how to use RWE, Mike, our mentor, introduced the four of us to it by involving us in its warrantied process (18, 7). Our exploration by experiencing it firsthand discovered that

✓ Whatever our senses experience in Nature is a self-evident fact for us in that moment, a fact that we have no need to defend because self-evidence is undeniable (18).
✓ We could reasonably see that we had many more than five senses operating because we experienced, spoke, and identified some of them: hearing, distance, gravity, self, language, consciousness, aliveness, humor, contrast, and reason (6).
✓ We could validate that nowhere here or anywhere else could we find any evidence of Nature communicating through stories or labels. Stories were an attribute of humanity alone (18).
✓ To help us know Nature as it knew its nameless and speechless self, we spent five minutes quietly in the woodland identifying each thing that we became aware of there as *nameless* or *story-less*. Attractive meaning and value were added to most things. We then got together and shared what we sensed and felt from doing this (22). We discovered that by dropping our labels and stories, what one person said they had experienced each of us sensed as well since we were still unified in and by the forest. This made sense to us because everything is a supportive part of Nature except our nature-disconnecting stories (17).

We helped each other realize that our love for or attraction to Nature that we were exploring was our 54 natural senses organically registering Albert Einstein's Higgs Boson Unified Attraction Field attracting all things into consciously belonging in the Universe's time and space of the moment (1, 11, 15). Then we soloed for the next five minutes while labeling everything we became aware of, including ourselves, as '*Unified Field Attraction Love*' (2).

When we came together again as a group, a stronger unifying feeling was undeniable. Now our senses of love, trust, place, community, and time became apparent as our forest community experience validated them (31). Folks spontaneously shared how this same feeling of well-being had helped them and others when they were ill or suffered disorders (12).

We noted that some folks addict to artificially producing this supportive feeling by using drugs, alcohol, or excessively dependent relationships. These detached them, short-term, from their abuse or nature-disconnecting stories and gave them relief or emotional rewards (3). However, these satisfactions were accompanied by detrimental aftereffects. RWE could replace this short circuit by its nature-affirming side-effects supporting, rather than injuring, the health of the natural world in and around us continually (4, 5).

The things we discovered from this RWE experience were

- ✓ How amazingly diverse Nature was,
- ✓ How we loved being aware of and in Nature,
- ✓ How each thing in a natural area was a unique and attractive individual, including each of us,
- ✓ How it felt good that everything was right there to experience and love in the moment,
- ✓ That we felt relieved by not having to label things *'correctly'* or at all,
- ✓ That we found many wonderful new things about Nature by removing stories and labels from them and that this made us feel closer to them,
- ✓ That a *'brightening'* or vibrancy of things took place when we called them 'Nameless.' We could hear things we didn't hear moments earlier,
- ✓ Feeling greater belongingness to everything including each other when we called ourselves *'nameless,'*
- ✓ Our habitual meditation process benefited from a new unifying dimension,
- ✓ Calling human-built structures and effects *'blueprints'* made us feel more reasonably able to control them.

We validated that these discoveries were true for each of us because we experienced them, they were self-evident, they registered directly on our senses (19).

We walked back to the beginning of the trail labeling things we experienced as *nameless, love, attraction*, or *unified field* and felt a greater wholeness than when we started walking. Then, Mike had us pinch ourselves until it hurt so much that we stopped. We explored how our sense of pain was not negative; rather, it was an attraction. It was Nature's protective attraction that signaled us to find more satisfying and reasonable attractions (24). We recognized that our sensations of anxiety, depression and anguish, our senses 25-27, also make this contribution to our welfare (6), and we could achieve this at will through nature-connecting activities.

We validated that, moment-by-moment, everything was attractively connected and as one as part of each moment of the Universe's Unified Field (2, 23). When we consciously thought that plants or we were alive, the Earth and Universe also had to be and act alive for us because the essence of everything was identical Unified Field attraction in that moment, including what our aliveness sensed and felt (16).

We ended up looking at the life of clouds as they moved across the sky into beautiful new shapes, and we felt harmony and peace knowing we were doing the same thing with them and each other, no matter our cultural or genetic differences (9). We noted that people in the middle of a city could do this with clouds, parks, and weeds (14). Then Mike distributed sheets with the 54 senses listed on them and activities we could do to strengthen what we had just discovered (get one here for yourself (13).

What fascinated me was that using RWE, we learned all this through trustable experiences in Nature, the real thing, in less than two hours. This was because what we were learning we could sense and feel right there, around, and in us immediately. This was powerfully different from the isolation generated by words in a book or lecture, words that Nature could not even register no less consider.

RWE was enabling us to be whole life reality, not just to abstract it with stories right or wrong (21). We were sensing and feeling that we were helping our 54 natural senses remember what they already knew. It felt attractive to give them safe time and space to connect, catch-up, and coalesce with themselves as natural attractions in a natural area, space/time moments rather than closets.

We concluded by validating that in Nature, what we were attracted to was doing the attracting in a balanced way to keep united. This natural love-in unified us. I recognized that at my school, it would take a full year science and philosophy course to get the same results if this was even possible (10). Could an indoor course ever substitute for learning how Nature works from authentic Nature, the fountainhead of authority in how it works? (20).

> "My yoga practice benefits from this experiential moment in the awakening of how each observation lends itself to my deepening of sensory integration. What I have learned is that this process is multilayered. I learned that as many senses as I could identify, there were many more at play simultaneously. I learned that the mystery of my organic being is nurtured through my RWE sensory interactions with my Earth Body beingness whether or not I am consciously aware. Taking away this experience from me would lessen the totality of my being." ~ **RWE participant interaction**

Similar to not reversing our excessive stress and related disorders, after their workshop, the Directors did not continue with RWE, and Earth Misery increased everywhere.

> "After my initial '*interruption*,' the fish reorganize, come back into homeostasis as a school, and include me! I relax, pretending I have a swim bladder, noticing how the air inside of me adjusts my position in the water. Surrounded by them, I just '*became*' a fish, amazing. Instead of watching them, I become them and seem to move automatically with the school, or maybe they attune and move with me. Or maybe we are a superorganism and are all one, as a school, as the bay, as the planet, as the multiverse. It doesn't really matter that I decide which or none. I have been invited and accepted. What a gift! We live IN the life of Planet Earth. I felt like I was IN the

womb and amniotic waters of the earth while swimming in the warm bay and believe she has given birth to me countless times over." ~ **RWE participant interaction**

Conclusion

🎬 All below:

Workshop Member: *What special contributions can RWE make to reduce Earth Misery and increase total well-being?*

RWE is that contribution because it helps you habitually wear GTT glasses.

> "Joan, as I read your, '*Taking my stories away*,' I was left with everything just being. It gave me a sense of ease and my body relaxed.
>
> I believe that I can now take the lens of nature and place it over my view of things. It is basically a way to look at everything. If I feel upset or any kind of pain, I try and take the nature lens and *look* through it.
>
> I love taking a step back and seeing if I am missing something. Even though you say, 'I may be doing it 5% of the time'. You also say that, '*Change takes time,*' and maybe someday you won't need a lens, but it will be your new eyesight.
>
> There is a part of me that now realizes I am significant and can make a difference around me and inside me. It seems that one way you are indeed making a difference is the quality of time you now spend with your kids."
> ~ **RWE participant interaction**

Like most people, the scientist that tried to help Jack stop his boat from leaking did not know the science of RWE. Teaching Jack RWE would have empowered him to learn from the water in the boat how to fill the holes in his head so he could fill the holes in the boat as well as become more whole. That is because the RWE teacher is 78-sensible Unified Field wisdom, moment by moment.

The natural wisdom of the water knew how to come into balance, that's what it was doing by gushing through the holes. It was not excessive. It's GTT knew to stop when the water in the boat reached the same level as the water around the boat. Similarly, the intelligence of our sense of thirst bringing water into us is not excessive when it does not have advertising, sugar, or drugs influencing it.

Our increasing Earth Misery demonstrates that Jack, in his box, the Earth Misery house that he/we build, cannot increase personal, social, and environmental well-being simply by *thinking outside of the box*. Instead, we must learn how to get out of the box by letting the story of RWE help us help each other get out of it. That involves adding RWE/GTT to whatever we do, especially what we love.

To our loss, education, counseling, and healing omit to teach how to get consent from a natural area to help us eco-love ourselves into being happy by reversing Earth Misery.

If you don't engage in RWE, what you learned here may make you more interesting at a cocktail party, or it could stress you along with the rest of us into additional Earth Misery.

Now is the only time and space that you can choose to begin to RWE improve your life. Now contains the essence of tomorrow. Now is the only time you can have your excellent childhood.

If you do learn or teach RWE, you may help Climate Therapy make 54-sense space for the Unified Field to:

- Stop the lies and corruption that infiltrate our lives so that we may take a *quantum leap* into a perfect union.

- Reduce the health insurance premiums of those who engage in RWE while reducing the health costs of insurance companies.
- Be profitably offered by the pharmaceutical and medical profession as a potent preventative and to hasten recovery from many disorders.
- Reduce the human service budgets of municipalities while improving personal, social, and environmental health.
- Make GTT contributions to conflict resolution on local and global levels.
- Improve the economy by reducing environmental costs and adding environmental recycling and health benefits.
- Give added value to natural areas to help industrial society's story come into balance with natural systems within and about us.
- Strengthen mental health by relieving our stress from Earth Misery as we transform it into love.
- Increase the responsibility and profitability of organizations that incorporate RWE into their management and operation.
- Produce a whole new human services economy that trains people to use, teach, and reap the benefits of RWE.

Real-life witnesses at a metaphor grand jury investigation about academia's Ivory Tower omission of RWE (25) testified that the Climate Therapy of RWE mental health:

- improves the quality, rights, and well-being of life,
- strengthens our ability to make beneficial changes,
- enhances equality through wholeness,
- bolsters appropriateness of education,
- strengthens mental health of body mind and spirit,
- reinforces the scientific truth of natural love,
- increases love and common good to stop corruption,
- heightens self-appreciation and sensory awareness
- strengthens our trust in scientific methodology,
- strengthens whole life equality,
- enhances pain reduction,
- reduces fear, negativity, and depression,
- intensifies harmony and our right to be loved,

- supports personal and global aliveness,
- strengthens the sense and vision of unity,
- increases intelligent attraction consciousness,
- restores the wisdom of reasonable happiness,
- affirms our right to demand whole life facts anywhere,
- sustains us lovingly communicating with the eons,
- reinforces our safe personal rejuvenation,
- invigorates organically based critical thinking,
- supports our healing attraction to an emotional place,
- unchains our inborn ability to love all of life,
- reverses our trespasses of Nature in and around us,
- heightens self-nourishing and supportive energies
- reduces our addictive prejudice against Nature,
- empowers recuperation from post-traumatic stress,
- enables sensing ourselves as the Unified Field,
- institutionally increases people/planet sanity.

"The part of me that was lacking in the past was my ability to validate and be present in the moment to understand the Now Attraction that I found in a natural area was/is that same attraction in me loving the joy of reuniting with itself and its unified family origins in that moment. I was able to bear witness to the Earth Misery and hold that place of compassion and also feel that deep, deep sadness and despair. I was feeling that and being in the moment with UNE was like having my umbilical reconnected to Earth. It gave me an understanding of how I have been not showing up and hiding myself when UNE were welcoming me and had the stage set for me to engage and be present in the moment where that presence could literally feed my whole ecosystem of my life. The Now Attraction also ignited a fire within me to use my unique gifts, skills, and power for the greater good of UNE and help heal Earth Misery." ~ **RWE participant interaction**

🎥 A good place to start RWE is (26) <ecopsych.com/LNE.html>

References

SUMMARY: RWE makes "Do unto others as you would have others do unto you" a reality by scientifically transforming "others" into love that includes the natural world.

1   *A new Copernican revolution.* (2012). Journal of Organic Psychology and Natural Attraction Ecology, 2. Retrieved from http://www.ecopsych.com/journalcopernicus.html

2   *Albert Einstein's unified field equation.* (2014-2016). Journal of Organic Psychology and Natural Attraction Ecology, 2. Retrieved from http://www.ecopsych.com/journalaliveness.html

3   Cohen, M. J. (1983). *Prejudice Against Nature.* Cobblesmith Retrieved from http://www.ecopsych.com/prejudicebigotry.html

4   Cohen, M. J. (1993) *The training ground of a nature-connected expert.* (2014). Retrieved from http://www.ecopsych.com/mjcohen.html

5   Cohen, M. J. (1995). *Education and counseling with nature: A greening of psychotherapy.* The Interspsych Newsletter, 2(4). Retrieved from http://www.ecopsych.com/counseling.html

6   Cohen, M. J. (1997). *Reconnecting With Nature,* EcoPress. Retrieved from http://www.ecopsych.com/insight53senses.html

7   Cohen, M. J. (2007a). *Thinking and feeling, and relating through the joy of nature's perfection.* Retrieved from http://www.ecopsych.com/naturepath.html

8   Cohen, M. J. (2008). *Educating, counseling, and healing with nature.* Illumina. Retrieved from http://www.ecopsych.com/ksanity.html

9   Cohen, M. J. (2010). *Planet Earth is a Living Organism.* Retrieved from http://www.ecopsych.com/livingplanetearthkey.html

10   Cohen, M. J. (2011). *The anatomy of institutions.* Retrieved from http://www.ecopsych.com/journalinstitution.html

11   Cohen, M. J. (2013). *The great Einstein sensory equation dance.* Retrieved from http://www.ecopsych.com/journalgut.html

12   Cohen, M. J. (2015). *A Survey of Nature-connected learning participants.* Retrieved from http://www.ecopsych.com/survey.html

13   Cohen, M. J. (2016). *Maverick Genius Walk.* Retrieved from http://www.ecopsych.com/MAKESENSEWALK.docx

14   Grange #966, (2015) *Resolutions,* Retrieved from http://www.sjigrange.wordpress.com/resolutions

15   Green, B. (2013). *How the Higgs Boson Was Found* Smithsonian Magazine, Retrieved from http://www.smithsonianmag.com/science-nature/how-the-higgs-boson-was-found-4723520/?cmd=ChdjYS1wdWItMjY0NDQyNTI0NTE5MDk0Nw&page=3

16   *Our living universe: Who is the boss of you?* (2014). Retrieved from http://www.ecopsych.com/universealive.html

17   *The hidden organic remedy: Nature as a higher power.* (2013). Journal of Organic Psychology and Natural Attraction Ecology, 1. Retrieved from http://www.ecopsych.com/nhpbook.html

18   *The impossible dream: We ask you to be a part of it.* (2011-2013). Journal of Organic Psychology and Natural Attraction Ecology, 1. Retrieved from http://www.ecopsych.com/journalwarranty.html

19   The National Grange. (1874, February 11). *The declaration of purposes of the National Grange,* Retrieved from http://www.oocities.org/cannongrange/declaration_purposes.html

20   *The state of planet earth and us.* (2001). Retrieved from http://www.ecopsych.com/zombie2.html

21   *Thinking and learning with all nine legs.*
(2011). Retrieved from   http://www.ecopsych.com/nineleg.html

22   Cohen, M. J. (2009a). *How to transform destructive thinking into constructive relationships.* Retrieved from http://www.ecopsych.com/transformation.html

23   Cohen, M. J. (2017). *How to Change our Disorders into Nature's Self-Correcting Way.* Retrieved from http://www.ecopsych.com/GREENWAVE.docx

24   Mallory, S. *Transforming Pain into Love Through Sensory Connections with Nature.* Retrieved from http://www.ecopsych.com/journalproposal.html

25   Cohen, M.J. *With Justice for All.* Retrieved from http://www.ecopsych.com/grandjury.html

26   Cohen, M. J. (2018). *How to Liberate Your Natural Essence.* Retrieved from http://www.ecopsych.com/LNE.html

27   Powell, C. S. *January 1, 1925: The Day We Discovered the Universe.* Retrieved from http://blogs.discovermagazine.com/outthere/2017/01/02/the-day-we-discovered-the-universe/#.XdDAZK3MyZM

28   Cohen, M. J. (2017). *The Scientific Core of all Known Relationships: Attraction is Conscious of What it is Attracted to.* Retrieved from www.ecopsych.com/66IJMRA-11702.pdf

29   Cohen, M. J. (2017). *The Global Wellness and Unity Activity.* Retrieved from www.ecopsych.com/amental.html.

30 Cohen, M. J. (2017). *An Earth Day or Any Day Activity for Therapists, Counselors, Coaches, and You.*
. Retrieved from http://www.ecopsych.com/giftearthday1.html

31 Cohen, M. J. (2017). *Nature Connected Health and Wellness Research.* Retrieved from http://www.ecopsych.com/2004ecoheal.html

32 *NY* Times (2019) *The Earth Is Just as Alive as You Are.* April 4, 2019: https://www.nytimes.com/2019/04/20/opinion/sunday/amazon-earth-rain-forest-environment.html

33 Cohen, M. J. (2017) *Smile! You're on Mindread Camera-78.* Retrieved from www.ecopsych.com/mindread.html

34 Hoke, P. (2015) Maverick *Genius at Work, You be the Judge.* Retrieved from http://www.ecopsych.com/think3genius.html

35 Reich, D. *The Fibonacci Sequence, Spirals, and the Golden Mean.* Retrieved from https://math.temple.edu/~reich/Fib/fibo.html

36 (1999) Murchie, *Seven Mysteries of Life.* Mariner Books

37 (1963) Cannon, *Wisdom of the Body.* W. W. Norton Company

38 (2012) Krutch *Voice of the Desert.* General Books

39 (1982) Cohen, *Our Secret Undeclared War With Nature* Retrieved from http://www.ecopsych.com/war.html

APPENDIX A: 54 SENSE LIST

Our Fifty-Four Natural Senses and Sensitivities

Living and learning as if the life of Nature matters

This list explains how, sense by sense in 54-sense resonance, RWE connects with and unifies itself in us, through us and with people and places around us. By putting these senses into scientific stories and labels the list enables our sense of language (sense #39) to consciously (sense #42) and reasonably (sense #43) translate into and engage in reasonable stories that connect us to the life and love of Nature/Earth's moment-by-moment, self-correcting survival process (sense #54). Climate Therapy is the outcome of the author's 51 years of living this organic experience in natural area space and time with his scientifically trained, evidence-based knowledge and awareness.

Full information: www.ecopsych.com/insight53senses.html

Key books that, in congress, validate this 54-sense list:

-*Seven Mysteries of Life* by Guy Murchie (36)
-*Wisdom of the Body* by Walter B. Cannon (37)
-*Voice of the Desert* by Joseph Wood Krutch (38)

IMPORTANT NOTE: Our isolated story way of knowing too often trespasses a natural area's integrity. However, a natural attraction there lasting for 7 seconds or more signals that attraction's consent for us to visit it.

Full information: www.ecopsych.com/amental.html

THE LIST OF 54 SENSES

The Radiation Senses
1. Sense of height and sight, including polarized light.
2. Sense of seeing without eyes such as heliotropism or the sun sense of plants.

3. Sense of color.

4. Sense of moods and identities attached to colors.

5. Sense of awareness of one's visibility or invisibility and consequent camouflaging.

6. Sensitivity to radiation other than visible light, including radio waves, X rays, etc.

7. Sense of Temperature and temperature change.

8. Sense of season, including the ability to insulate, hibernate, and winter sleep.

9. Electromagnetic sense and polarity which includes the ability to generate current (as in the nervous system and brain waves) or other energies.

The Feeling Sense

10. Hearing including resonance, vibrations, sonar, and ultrasonic frequencies.

11. Awareness of pressure, particularly underground, underwater, and to wind and air.

12. Sensitivity to gravity.

13. The sense of excretion for waste elimination and protection from enemies.

14. Feel, particularly touch on the skin.

15. Sense of weight, gravity, and balance.

16. Space or proximity sense.

17. Coriolus sense or awareness of effects of the rotation of the Earth.

18. Sense of motion. Body movement sensations and a sense of mobility.

The Chemical Senses

19. Smell with and beyond the nose.

20. Taste with and beyond the tongue.

21. Appetite or hunger for food, water, and air.

22. Hunting, killing, or food obtaining urges.

23. Humidity sense including thirst, evaporation control, and the acumen to find water or evade a flood.

24. Hormonal sense, as to pheromones and other chemical stimuli.

The Mental Senses

(25 -27 are attractions that 'say' (attract us to) seek additional natural attractions to support well-being.)

25. **Pain, external, and internal.**
26. **Mental or spiritual distress.**
27. **Sense of fear, dread of injury, death, or attack**
28. Procreative urges: sex awareness, courting, love, mating, paternity, and raising young.
29. Sense of play, sport, humor, pleasure, and laughter.
30. Sense of physical place, navigation senses including detailed awareness of land and seascapes, of the positions of the sun, moon, and stars.
31. Sense of time and rhythm.
32. Sense of electromagnetic fields.
33. Sense of weather changes.
34. Sense of emotional place, of community, belonging, support, trust, and thankfulness.
35. Sense of self, including friendship, companionship, and power.
36. Domineering and territorial sense.
37. Colonizing sense including compassion and receptive awareness of one's fellow creatures, sometimes to the degree of being absorbed into a superorganism.
38. Horticultural sense and the ability to cultivate crops, as is done by ants that grow fungus, by fungus who farm algae or birds that leave food to attract their prey.

(39, 42, 43 are the CRL core of Organic Psychology)

39. **Language and articulation sense** used to express feelings and convey information in every medium from the bees' dance to human stories and literature.
40. Sense of humility, appreciation, ethics.
41. Senses of form and design.
42. **Sense of Reason,** including memory and the capacity for logic and science.
43. **Sense of Mind and Consciousness**.

44. Intuition or subconscious deduction.

45. Aesthetic sense, including creativity and appreciation of beauty, music, literature, form, design, and drama.

46. Psychic capacity such as foreknowledge, clairvoyance, clairaudience, psychokinesis, astral projection, and possibly certain animal instincts and plant sensitivities.

47. Sense of biological and astral time, awareness of past, present, and future events.

48. The capacity to hypnotize other creatures.

49. Relaxation and sleep, including dreaming, meditation, brainwave awareness.

50. Sense of pupation, including cocoon building and metamorphosis.

51. Sense of excessive stress and capitulation.

52. Sense of survival by joining a more established organism.

53. Spiritual sense, including conscience, capacity for sublime love, ecstasy, a sense of sin, profound sorrow, and sacrifice.

54. Sense of whole life unity, of natural attraction as the singular, *love of love* essence of all our other senses (and everything else that singularity was and remains attracted to create, unify and support, moment-by-moment, as Einstein's Big Bang Unified Field (Higgs Boson, that was verified in 2012 A.D.).

APPENDIX B: Twenty-Four RWE Indisputable Facts

Basic Understanding

A. Nature loves to create and live its life moment by moment. Its life as Planet Earth's natural areas does not have the ability to create or understand stories and their outcomes.

B. Humanity is 54-sense Nature in the life of Planet Earth that has the natural ability to create, share and be guided by story abstract-shortcuts.

> Nature-connective, evidence-based stories that supportively attach people to Nature are constructive. They are Nature as people.

> Nature-disconnecting stories that excessively separate Humanity from Nature are abusive to people and Nature. They produce Earth Misery

C. **RWE Climate Therapy** in natural areas consists of creating and acting-out nature-connecting stories that help us increae well-being and reduce Earth Misery.

* * * * *

We suffer our disorders because our half-truths injure the reasonable passion of our 54-senses to support the life of Earth/us. These 54 intelligences are eleven times more astute, powerful, sensitive, unifying, and responsible than our *normal*, 5-sense ways and means of relating.

RWE validates when and why evidence-based natural area contacts beneficially add the undeniable organic truths of 54-sense science to our arts, loves, and thinking. Its therapeutic process creates hands-on moments that let the stricken life of Earth generate responsible healing and joy for itself and us.

1. **Now attraction RWE essence.** The essence of all things is the singular now attraction energy of Einstein's unified field.
2. **Fittest most cooperative.** The fittest things are the most attractive cooperators with other things.

3. **Life of GTT/ RWE undeniable.** Self-evident truth is alive, undeniable, and scientifically valid, yet it is not God, Nature, Love, Life, or Honesty.

4. **GTT/ RWE is us evidence-based, experiencing our life in the now.**

5. **Now is film frame mist life:**
   As per www.ecopsych.com/journalmist.html, the now is the life of the *"immediate moment, space/time, film-frame, the mist of our expanding, love-balloon universe"* (Now. *capital N*).

6. **The life of RWE wants to live.** The life of Nature and Earth is attracted to continue to live, *to survive* into the next moment

7. **Natural area attractions are them in us being homesick.** Now attraction that we find in a natural area is that same attraction in us loving the joy of reuniting with itself and its unified family origins in the area.

8. **The life of the RWE Big Bang never dies.** Since its life was born, the Universe/Nature has remained alive.

9. **The Now is RWE making its time and space.** All things only exist or happen to us in the Now. It is the instant when the Universe makes its own time and space, moment-by-moment.

10. **We are fiduciaries in Gaia/Us**. We live in the life of Planet Earth, as fiduciaries of it and each other.

11. **Attraction is free will conscious of what attracts it to hold RWE's life together**. Since the beginning, Natural attraction has been free will conscious of what it is attracted to, and everything is held together by that attraction.

12. **All things in the Now Film Frame are attached to all past and future things.** Anything and everything is attached to all that has gone before it and all that follows it. All are always present in the Now as the Golden Ratio.

13. **There are no repulsions, negatives, or prejudices in UNE life;** it singularly consists of its stronger or weaker attraction-love dance.

14. **Homeostatic balance: every film frame is simultaneously attracted to its present and future life.** For every new-moment natural attraction in the Now, there is an equal, central, natural attraction to support the life of that Film Frame. This is the balance of natural homeostasis

15. **The awareness screen of Consciousness can register our 54 natural senses.** We have at least 54 Now natural sense groups that register their attraction relationships in our sense of consciousness (#42).

16. **Nothing in RWE knows or relates via stories except people.** In the life-web of Planet Earth, except for humanity, nothing uses or understands our verbalized, literate-story way of knowing (#39).

17. **Spirit/Love/God attraction is found everywhere.** Spirit, creation, self, or God are our organic love-of-love (sense #54) that is found everywhere in the Now of a natural area and us.

18. **Identifying our 78 sensibilities in Groks increase wellness.** Identifying our 54-senses/24- facts by name in our Groks makes a critically unique contribution that increases well-being.

19. **Unifying people's GTT/RWE stories catalyzes healing.** The art of creating scientifically accurate, 54-sense stories that are supported by other people's GTT/RWE stories, is needed to catalyze organic change or healing.

20. **CRL creates reasonable human relationships**. GreenWave-54 Grokking via our Consciousness, Reason, and Literacy senses creates organically sound human relationships.

21. **Things must be valued or measured by their effects.**

22. **RWE abuse pain avoidance creates abusive relationships.** We often avoid re-living the pain of what has abused us by the relief and satisfactions gained from abusing others as we were abused, or by co-dependent relationships and/or addictively tranquilizing it.

23. **Omitting GTT/ RWE creates Earth Misery**. Commencing in 1974, and similar to omitting the full value of an equation numeral, omitting any of the above facts, transforms GTT/RWE into Earth Misery until the omission is GTT corrected.

24. **Co-mentoring GTT Groks transforms Earth Misery into RWE**. In a natural area, we can co-mentor and transform Earth Misery into the therapeutic well-being of Revolutionary Wisdom.

APPENDIX C: The Gospel of Forty Days

In the brave pioneering love and spirit of the scientific truth that she contributes to the world (24), the book's editor, Dr. Stacey S. Mallory, observed that I include the following quote in this book, and she has asked me to validate its rationale and authenticity.

> Jesus said, "The Kingdom of God is inside/within you, and all about you, and as you, not in buildings/mansions of wood and stone or fabricated stories. When I am gone, hug a tree, and I am there. Split a wooden stick, and I am there. Lift [the]a stone and me being you will find us." ~ **PNC Gospel of Forty Days** *(updated from the Gospel of Thomas)*

An actuality of *Climate Therapy* is that for the past 55 years, my life has centered around my 1965 discovery that the life of Earth and myself is/are identical except that I can verbally tell stories, and it can't. This was preceded by 20 years dedicated to seeking that *Planet Earth is alive* moment and includes, since 1990, nine thousand daily trips up Young Hill in the protected natural areas of San Juan Island National Historical Park. This seventy-five-year total period includes the past 50 years sleeping outdoors year-round and founding Ph.D. quality, nature-connected education, counseling and healing with Nature programs. My neighbors who see me do my walks to and from the National Park can attest to this almost daily-trip event being true. See <www.ecopsych.com/mjcohen.html>.

In my quest to reduce Earth Misery and help others do the same, during these 9,000+ hours of natural area walks, I developed and practiced the eco-arts and science of RWE. It includes my 54-sense awareness that my attraction to do this is conscious of this attraction;

- the three-decade daily phenomenon scientifically takes place IN Planet Earth's UNE time/space moment-by-moment when the essence of all things is/are identical including my stories and felt-sense experiences;
- the event is always attached to all that has preceded and will follow it;

- my medical exams show I have not aged much during these 30 years; and
- at 90 years of age, I'm not on any medications.

While on these walks, I am aware that whatever takes place is UNE reality, and during them, I have conscious contact with whatever comes to mind or takes place. This includes the similar periods that Jesus, Moses, Joseph Smith, and many others spent *40-something time* in natural areas and I explore their experiences as part of my own knowing they are identical with this major exception. The story world did not include the scientific existence of the Big Bang Unified Field Universe until 1925 and the light bulb was not invented until 1880. These major leaders did not know how to change a bulb, use, or repair modern technology, or that the catastrophe of Earth Misery is real, that their lives existed only because the life of UNE existed, or that God and the supernatural are not evidence-based reality. For this reason, I spend some time on my walks explaining to these icons how and why the art of science works in hopes that they may help their followers wake up to this reality and the contribution made by Climate Therapy rather than deny all these facts that Camera Film-78 corroborates.

In answer to Dr. Mallory's question, during my natural area walks, these spiritual leaders and I unite in, and as, identical kin in the life of the Unified Field. I am the person Jesus addresses in the quote. I extended the ancient *agnostic* scrolls of Thomas and Apocrypha in order to contribute 54-sense reasonableness to the senseless parts of today's world and to strengthen Climate Therapy. Also, since the Unified Field and Big Bang exist, I produced for them their own unique *Gospel of Forty Days*. It helps them reduce prejudice and enjoy the fairness of equal footing in the critical quest to reduce our abusiveness and reverse Earth Misery.

On the other hand, as Sinclair Lewis noted: ***"A man who was merely a man and said the sort of things Jesus said wouldn't be a great moral teacher. He'd be either a lunatic on a level with a man who says he's a poached egg or else he'd be the devil of hell."***

For UNE justice I may madly turn thief and poach a deviled egg. ☺

Appendix D: How to Utilize this Book

Congratulations, the life of Nature and Planet Earth is attracted to you being here. Whenever our story world employs Nature as a resource without its consent, it hurtfully abuses GTT/RWE around, within, and as us, so we suffer, and we must reasonably recover from these injuries. This phenomenon occurs on global, local, and personal levels and this book helps be and provide a unique, organic resolution for this dilemma that peacefully creates beautiful, pure, and balanced relationships.

Here are things you can do to with this book:

Involve yourself in beneficially applying what was attractive to you here *www.ecopsych.com/LNE.html*

Help others download it, (donation required) at *http://www.ecopsych.com/climatetherapy.pdf*

Obtain a softcover copy. **Google:** *Amazon.com How to Liberate Your Natural Essence: The Art and Science of Sensory Validation,* **Michael J. Cohen. Note: This book is also available at other major online book stores and in various libraries.**

Obtain this **book as an accredited, softcover,** CEU professional and academic course workbook *A Nature Lovers Path to Peace.* Michael J. Cohen *https://www.amazon.com*

Help your arts and interests be therapeutic for others:

http://ecoart-therapy.org/courses/
www.ecopsych.com/orient.html

Use this book as the core of a **certificate or nature-connected degree training program and community** *www.ecopsych.com/LNE.html.*

Become eligible for a subsidized, **18-month BS, MS, or Ph.D.** online, autobiographical, nature-connected degree program that strengthens your special love, interest, or skill.
www.ecopsych.com/18month.html

Social Network the following page

Learn or Teach Heartfelt Eco-Arts Therapy
Let your loves and skills help others. Subsidized training available online.

Nature: Do you ( ) enjoy ( ) like ( ) love Nature?

Arts & Skills: List one or more that you love _____.

Fine Art   Drawing   Yoga   Friending   Science   Horses
Writing   Healing   Gardening   Psychology   Recovery   Music
Teaching   Pets   Human Services   Parenting   Acting
Ecotherapy   Other

Apply for a Waiver/Volunteer Work-Study to assist you with the cost of courses, certificates, or degrees.
http://ecoart-therapy.org/courses/

Project NatureConnect (PNC)
P. O. Box 1605, Friday Harbor, WA, 98250
1-360-378-6313   nature@interisland.net
www.projectnatureconnect.com

Made in the USA
Columbia, SC
23 February 2020